ALL
IS BUT A
BEGINNING

Books by John G. Neihardt published by the UNP

ALL IS BUT A BEGINNING: YOUTH REMEMBERED, 1881–1901 (Cloth and BB)

BLACK ELK SPEAKS: BEING THE LIFE STORY OF A HOLY MAN OF THE OGLALA SIOUX (Cloth)

LYRIC AND DRAMATIC POEMS (BB 322)

THE MOUNTAIN MEN (Vol. I of A CYCLE OF THE WEST) (BB 531)

THE RIVER AND I (BB 378)

THE SPLENDID WAYFARING. THE EXPLOITS AND ADVENTURES OF JEDEDIAH SMITH AND THE ASHLEY-HENRY MEN, 1822–1831 (BB 525)

THE TWILIGHT OF THE SIOUX (Vol. II of A CYCLE OF THE WEST) (BB 532)

WHEN THE TREE FLOWERED: THE FICTIONAL AUTOBIOGRAPHY OF EAGLE VOICE, A SIOUX INDIAN (BB 526)

ALL
IS BUT A
BEGINNING

Youth Remembered, 1881–1901

JOHN G. NEIHARDT

Introduction by
DICK CAVETT

University of Nebraska Press
Lincoln and London

First Bison Book printing: 1986
Most recent printing indicated by the first digit below:
1 2 3 4 5 6 7 8 9 10

Library of Congress Cataloging-in-Publication Data
Neihardt, John Gneisenau, 1881–1973
  All is but a beginning.
  Reprint. Originally published: New York: Harcourt
Brace Jovanovich, [1972]
  1. Neihardt, John Gneisenau, 1881–1973—Biography—
Youth. 2. Authors, American—20th century—Biography.
3. Frontier and pioneer life—West (U.S.) 4. West
(U.S.)—Description and travel—1880–1950. I. Title.
PS3527.E35Z464 1986   811'.52 [B]   85-28955
ISBN 0-8032-3312-4
ISBN 0-8032-8355-5 (pbk.)

Reprinted by arrangement with Hilda Neihardt Petri, Trustee, the
John G. Neihardt Trust.

The lines from "The Ghostly Brother" and "Child's Heritage" are
reprinted from *Lyric and Dramatic Poems* by John G. Neihardt by
permission of University of Nebraska Press, copyright 1913 by *Poetry:
A Magazine of Verse,* copyright 1915 by *The Forum,* copyright 1915,
1916, 1919, 1921, 1926, and 1926 by The Macmillan Company,
renewal copyright 1954 by John G. Neihardt. The lines from "The
Song of Jed Smith," "The Song of Hugh Glass," and "The Song of
Three Friends" are reprinted from *The Mountain Men* by John G.
Neihardt by permission of University of Nebraska Press, copyright
1915, 1919, 1941, 1949 by The Macmillan Company, copyright 1943,
1946, 1953 by John G. Neihardt. The lines from "The Song of the
Messiah" are reprinted from *The Twilight of the Sioux* by John G.
Neihardt by permission of University of Nebraska Press, copyright
1925, 1935, 1949 by The Macmillan Company, copyright 1943, 1946,
1953 by John G. Neihardt.

This testament of youth
is dedicated to
my grandchildren:

Joan, Elaine, Nei, Mona, Maxine,
Gail, Lynn, Robin, Erica and Coralie

And to my great-grandchildren:

Bobby, Janet, Joanna, Scott, Nei,
Lisa, Alexis and Chris

And to any other "Wubs" who may yet come
to share this planet with us.

With abiding love from

GAKI

Introduction

This book is an account of the early years in the life of an extraordinary man. It tells of a time well before his own achievements reflected the man, and long before honors recognized those achievements.

John Gneisenau Neihardt was born almost a decade before the close of the Indian Wars, and I can never get my mind around this and the fact that *I* know him. Or that I once sat in a quiet Nebraska living room on a Sunday afternoon, sipping beer with a man who, after talking about his impressions of the televised moon walk, could begin the next sentence with, "When I was deckhand to Captain Marsh on the *Expansion* . . ." Because of something I had just read I realized, with a jolt, that he meant Captain Grant Marsh, whose steamer *The Far West* brought home the wounded survivors of Major Reno's command after the Custer battle. It was a few moments before I regained my equilibrium.

John was born on January 8, 1881, near Sharpsburg, Illinois. In 1886 the family moved to the upper Solomon River in Kansas, and two years later to Kansas City. Eighteen ninety-one found them in Wayne, Nebraska, where John attended the Nebraska Normal College, completing the scientific course in 1897, at the age of sixteen.

At twelve, John began to experience the strange and recurring dream-vision that was to change the course of his life. Until then, his ambition had been to become a great inventor, but the dream—akin, perhaps, to the power visions of the Indian medicine men he was to know in later life—seemed to urge and steer him toward poetry, and before he was thirteen he had written two epic poems in blank verse. And mysticism lured him. He came to hold the belief that a dynamic spiritual pattern is at work in the cosmos, and that a man's destiny is spelled out in such a pattern.

While still in his teens, John completed a work based on Oriental philosophy, with the precocious title *The Divine Enchantment.* It was his first published work. Copies of this book are extremely rare and valuable today, their rarity having been increased when the author—in a burst of extreme self-criticism—committed to the flames every copy he could get his hands on. (If you find one, grab it!)

In this new book, *All Is But a Beginning,* John has chosen to tell of his early youth up to the end of the last century, when he had reached nineteen. Just at that time, he became deeply interested in the culture, folklore, and religion of the American Indian. He had been teaching in a country school near Hoskins, Nebraska, a small town not far from the Omaha Indian Reservation, and it was there, working with an Indian trader for thirty dollars a month, that he made his first close friendships with the Indians. His intensifying interest in their highly developed spiritual life led ultimately to his now famous *Black Elk Speaks.*

That book has an interesting history. After a listless send-off by its first publisher, *Black Elk Speaks* virtually vanished for a generation until the renowned philosopher and psychologist Carl Jung came across a copy in Zurich and caused it to be translated into German. News of its European renaissance brought the book back to life in America.

Readers of *Black Elk Speaks* know the remarkable story of how it came to be. John journeyed to the cabin of the aging Sioux holy man near Manderson, South Dakota, in 1930. Although the visit was unannounced, the old man seemed to have been expecting him. As they sat on the ground and talked, Black Elk became convinced that John had been sent by the Grandfathers (the great spirits of the universe) to record his story. Announcing that he sensed "in this man a desire to know the things of the Other World," Black Elk invited John to return when the grass was hand-high, at which time he would relate his life story so that it might be "preserved for men." It is the story of a mighty vision given to Black Elk when he was a young boy. In the vision, the great spirits of the universe carried the boy to the center of the earth and showed him all the good things in the Sacred Hoop of the Universe. Black Elk understood the vision as a sign that he should, through its power, lead his people back to a time of peace and plenty. Haunted by the feeling that he had failed at this sacred task, he hoped that through the preservation of his story, the Tree of the People could somehow still be brought to flower.

John's own highly developed sense of spiritual values harmonized thoroughly with that of the Indians. His uncanny ability to render into English not only the details but the spirit of the sacred tale, which was told to him by Black Elk in the Lakota tongue, has earned him the envy and admiration of scholars and ethnologists. But he told me that his greatest compliment came from one of the old long-hairs who proclaimed, "His heart is as Sioux as ours."

More than five thousand days, between the ages of thirty-one and sixty, were devoted to the fulfillment of a Neihardt dream: to produce an epic poem that would encompass the discovery, exploration, and settlement of the West. The sequence of poems, *A Cycle of the West,* starts in 1822 on the Missouri River and ranges westward until 1890, when the spirit and resistance of the Indians was crushed in the massacre at Wounded Knee.

Not all of John's work has been devoted to the West. In 1907 his collection of love poems, which he calls "rather frank for that time," was published under the title *A Bundle of Myrrh.* A young woman in Paris (I got the time-warp sensation again when he said to me, "My wife, who was studying sculpture with Rodin at the time . . .") discovered a copy, wrote to the author, and an epistolary romance began. She sailed the ocean, crossed the country by train, and arrived at the Omaha railroad depot, where young Neihardt waited with a marriage license in his hand. They were happily married until her death, fifty years later.

During his lifetime, John Neihardt has been the recipient of too many honors to list here. He has degrees from the University of Nebraska, the University of Missouri, and Creighton University. In 1921, by an act of the Nebraska State Legislature, he was awarded the title of Poet Laureate, which he retains to this day. The National Poetry Center awarded him the medal of honor as foremost poet of the nation in 1936.

In 1923 he was appointed professor of poetry at the University of Nebraska. In addition to creative writing and teaching, he distinguished himself in journalism, serving as literary editor of the Minneapolis *Journal,* the Kansas City *Journal,* and the St. Louis *Post-Dispatch.* In 1948 he became poet-in-residence and lecturer in English at the University of Missouri.

These are a few of his honors and achievements. Whether his ninety minutes on my television program belongs on this list, I am not sure. I only know that his appearance drew the kind of mail I had not received before, nor have I since. John is a born performer, and to hear such vivid and moving recollections from a ninety-one-year-old man, himself so thoroughly in the present, was a unique experience. His impact on the young was dynamic. They felt an instant kinship with a man who, chronologically, should be several generation gaps away. The appearance also resulted in still another rebirth of *Black Elk Speaks,* and renewed interest in the phenomenon of John G. Neihardt. Here are his recollections of his earliest years.

DICK CAVETT

ALL
IS BUT A
BEGINNING

1

There was no one yet, and it was nowhere. It was not even now, for time had not begun. Nor was there meaning in it, until memory awoke to re-create and question. Then I knew that it was I who saw the cozy flicker of the mysterious light, and felt the loving warmth glow all about me, and the strong hands beneath that kept me safe.

When, years later, I asked my Mother what such memories might mean, she said that must have been when we were visiting at the home of my Grandfather Neihardt in Indiana. "You were the baby," she said, "and your old Aunt Cass Phipps was very fond of you. I think she had been giving you a bath and she was warming your bare bottom by the fire on the hearth."

2

The foregoing stands as the momentous first chapter of a personal history I am writing for my family and friends, and for anybody else who may love me at least a little. Surely it is momentous, for it is a faithful account of my first awareness of this world; and what a propitious beginning for a life — that sense of loving strength and safety, and the pleasant warmth upon my bottom!

But, important as that earliest experience is, birth certainly came first; and here again I must rely upon hearsay, although I was present in person at the time.

Here then is the picture I have created, out of the little I have heard, by way of realizing how I ever got into this strange and awesome place where I have somehow managed to remain for ninety years:

It was the late evening of January 8, 1881, and it was cold. There had been a midwinter thaw. But now the muddy, rutted road was frozen hard again, and a raw wind was blowing out of the Northwest.

Not far from the little village of Sharpsburg, in the midst of the vast central Illinois plain, an old German woman with a featherbed upon her back was stumbling along the road in the deepening twilight. It is almost as though I had seen it all with my own eyes, the picture is so definitely drawn. She was headed for a little two-room house that I might have called a shack were it not for the wry gratitude I feel for my first shelter in this sometimes inhospitable world. There was soon going to be a new baby in that house, and the old woman was the welcoming committee. God bless her soul! I don't know who she was, but God should know the one I mean.

One look around the lamp-lit room within explained the featherbed, if what I've heard be true. The builder of that house had never got around to plastering, and the ventilating system must have been excellent. I can see the hip-supported chimney and the cast-iron cookstove with a stack of wood behind it and a steaming kettle on it. And I can see two little girls, all washed and starched as though for Sunday, sitting stiffly and expectant. They were my sisters—two and four years old—and they were dutifully obeying our Mother, who had dressed them when the pains began to worsen and told them they must be very good because a nice old lady was coming to see them.

4

Here the picture blurs like a rainy windowpane. Perhaps my Mother went no further with the story.

3

A casual reader who had never known my Mother might infer that I was born in most unbeautiful surroundings; but that would be a big mistake.

Had the old lady looked carefully about her in the dingy light of the coal-oil lamp, she could hardly have failed to notice esthetic details here and there. For instance, as I have heard, the windows were not bare, as might be supposed, but quite stylish with curtains made of newspapers neatly cut into fancy patterns. As for the floor, it was not bare either. It was nicely carpeted from wall to wall with a wagon cover that you could hardly tell from rich people's rugs because of the lovely patterns stamped upon it with the juice of green walnuts! And there was straw beneath the carpet to make for luxurious comfort and gracious living.

I have heard somehow of these and other marvels, and having known my Mother, I believe.

4

It has been noted that there is no trace of my Father in the picture I have created, a fact in keeping with all my memories of him; for he always was a mystery to me. Perhaps he had been out around the neighborhood—maybe as far as Taylorville—looking for some sort of paying job that would bring a little money in; and this was at a time, I have been told, when a silver dollar looked like the full moon in August and men were cheaper than money. Perhaps he had alerted the old lady, along with other preparations for the impending event.

In any case, I know he was glad that I happened to be a boy, for he gave me the most precious name he knew—John Greenleaf. I wore that name for some years, with scant appreciation of its import to my Father, I'm afraid. Then it became clear that I was going to be known as a poet, and so for Greenleaf I substituted a proud family name that bore the same initial—Gneisenau. (The first name was rightfully mine, being inherited from my paternal Grandfather.) Thus a warrior displaced a poet as my namesake; and reasonably enough, for were not Sword and Song companions in adventure from remote antiquity?

In this connection a family story that may well be more than rumor alleges that Neidhardt von Reuenthal, the Minnesinger, was of our breed; and it is a minor matter of history that he sang and fiddled his way with the knights to Damietta in the Fourth Crusade. I love that story, and I hope it's true. It thrills me, as beautiful swords have always thrilled me; and in either case I don't know why.

The first American Neihardts (Neidhardts originally) were George, Michael, and Caspar, three brothers, who came from the Rhenish Palatinate near Zweibruecken in 1737, settling in Pennsylvania. Fourteen of us fought in the Revolutionary War; and my Great-Great-Grandfather Christian was killed under Washington in the Battle of Long Island. These were the direct descendants of Hans, Ulrich, and Caspar Neithardt, who received a *Wappenbrief* from Maximilian ("der Roemische Koenig") at Mainz in 1140. Their coat of arms is described as "three barbed roses gules on a bend azure on a field gules." They were given large estates near Zweibruecken, which they held until the Thirty Years' War, when their lands were devastated and they were dispossessed and impoverished.

My Great-Grandfather Conrad crossed the Alleghenies after the war and settled in Wayne County, Ohio. My Grandfather John was born "in the year one," as he used to say

6

jokingly by way of indicating what an antique he had become. My Father was born in Sandusky in 1854, moving with the family to Indiana, where he grew up in the backwoods, the youngest of seventeen children. He spoke no English until he was eleven years old and his schooling must have been sketchy indeed, yet by the time I came along the greatest name he knew was Whittier's. Not that I ever heard him say the word so far as I can remember. In fact, I cannot recall the sound of his voice and do not actually remember his telling me anything. But as I dream back those ancient days, I realize that there are many things I came to know that no one else could possibly have told me. For instance, before I was ten years old I knew the names of Darwin, Huxley, and Robert G. Ingersoll. There was a strange power in the names, although I knew nothing of their significance; but along with the feeling of power they gave me was a troubling sense of something wrong about them, something somehow guilty that seemed to set my Father apart, making him lonely and different from other boys' fathers. And "different" he certainly was—even "queer" as neighbors must have seen him. There were times when I saw too clearly with their eyes and was cruelly torn between loyalty and shame.

For instance I can see him coming down Twenty-fifth Street in Kansas City to our home on Olive with the damnedest collection of broken-down buggies, rattling wagons, and crowbait horses ever assembled in one string! My Father was out of a job again, and knowing horses from his boyhood, he had invested his meager remaining capital in the hope of a quick and profitable turnover at the city horse market. I never knew how he came out; but I recall the whirlwind ride we took in a two-wheeled cart behind a "gilflirt" pacing mare whose infirmity, aggravated by her speed, doused us with spray!

For a day or two our back-yard clutter was the talk of the neighborhood. The kids made fun of it.

But it comforted me to know that my Father's "difference" could be fascinating, once we had left the town on our Sunday

7

wanderings. As an illustration, compare my memory of that ludicrous procession with the following: My Father was an incorrigible romantic, very fond of soldiers and soldiering, and once he took me out to a big army encampment, on the Sangamon, I think. There was target practice and there was drilling, and there were maneuvers. And then—

They formed along the brow of a low hill—a long line of mounted men in blue, with restless horses prancing and guidons flying. And a bugle sang, and a great cry went up, and the horses surged forward in a brisk trot that grew into a wild gallop, full of flying manes and tails and naked sabers flashing in the sun, and rolling thunder in the dust beneath!

It wasn't fear that made me feel like crying.

And afterward whole companies went swimming together, running with happy shouting down to the water, with their whangdoodles showing in a joyful riot of maleness!

Most of the Neihardt children were boys, a fact greatly pleasing to Grandma, who didn't have much use for girls. She was strictly a man's woman. Although I was a very little boy when I knew her, I still can see her plainly—but how much is memory and how much hearsay I do not know. I see a short, sturdily built, quick-moving little dynamo of a woman; and, according to all reports, she fairly bristled with "character." "Old Mrs. Neihardt" seems to have become a legendary figure in her own time and country. There is the saga of her discussion with a really dangerous but mistaken bull who had never had the pleasure of meeting my Grandma before. "He come at me," she is reported as saying, "but I don't run. I stay right there and beat him on the nose with my stick. He paw and he dung and he paw and he dung and he tear up the ground with his horns. So I beat him some more and I yell, '*Heraus mit dir!*' And he got!"

Then there was the time when Grandma was immobilized (in theory!) by the arrival of another baby. This occurred just a day before an especially important quilting bee was slated to be held in the neighborhood. "*Well!*" someone remarked sniffingly, "old Mrs. Neihardt won't be there *this*

time!" But, having heard the remark repeated, Grandma *was*
—and so was the baby!

Grandma Neihardt, I am proud to report, was a strictly
pious woman, and for that reason she was violently opposed
to sewing machines. It was clear to her that they were the
work of the Devil and symptomatic of what the godless world
was coming to. Sewing was a woman's business, like having
babies and cooking and baking and washing clothes and
hoeing the garden. What was a woman to do if Devil machines
took over her duties?

Grandma was very proud of her boys—thirteen or fourteen
of them, I believe. Some of them were old enough to be
fathers of the youngest, and some were older than my mater-
nal Grandfather. They had all disappeared when I knew her,
having fanned out across the Great West and Mexico, pioneering here and there all the way to Oregon, some shedding
the *d*'s and even the diphthong from their name as they went.
Some flourished and others just disappeared. One of my
uncles went into the Little Belt Mountains of Montana with
a pick and shovel and a burro, found a silver mine, and left
a little town to bear his name. Several of the older ones had
been killed in the Civil War. One died at Shiloh with a bullet
in his breast. His bloodstained coat with the hole in it was
sent home by his brother. Grandma hung it on the peg by
the kitchen door where the boy's coat used to hang. There it
stayed for years and years, they say.

5

When a man of my years begins remembering, Time ceases
to seem the orderly progression it is commonly supposed to
be and becomes a reservoir of contemporaneous voices and
echoes. *Thens* neighbor familiarly with *nows*, their changeless
pictures waiting in a motionless forever.

I see that I have wandered far from my birth, boldly remembering things that had not yet happened, according to our myth of Time. So now I find myself in Springfield at Fourth and Capitol Avenue. The new State House is slowly nearing completion, and many teams of horses, harnessed in a long string, are dragging one of the great stone columns down the street. It is riding on rollers that are being switched from rear to front as lathered horses squat and strain, leaning to the load, or plunge and bicker, inching forward down the avenue, whips cracking, men shouting.

I know that I was four years old at that time, or maybe a trifle older, because I can remember exactly where I stood with my Father when we heard from a shouting newsboy that a great man called Grant had died.

That was a golden year for me, as I recall it now. Along with the procession of the columns, I can see men and horses working on the grounds of the Lincoln Memorial. There for the first time I knew the spell of awe, inspired, no doubt, by what my Father must have told me. It did not seem to be about a man at all. It was something still and sad and everywhere, and waiting, always waiting.

But it was not only the procession of the columns and the waiting monument that made the year a golden one for me. Anyone who can recall his first grand passion will understand the way it was with me that year when I was four.

Her name was *Etta Stadden!*

Say it slowly; say it over and over very softly until you hear the lovely music of it! I can almost hear it yet the way it sounded then, and there's so much I've heard and can no longer hear.

Etta Stadden! Etta Stadden!

She must have been a very pretty little girl from all I can remember.

Her eyes were big and soft and brown.

There was a way she walked.

There was a way she said just anything at all.

She had such pretty bright hair.

Her eyes were big and soft and brown.

Her name was *Etta Stadden, Etta Stadden!*

My Father had managed to go into business somehow, and so we had a little grocery store on the corner of Fourth and Capitol. Down the avenue, a short distance toward the State House, there was a bridge across the street, and it was underneath that bridge we met. It was love at first sight, and she took me to her home nearby to see her mother, whose eyes were also big and soft and brown. And she was always sewing, because they needed money and their father was dead. He was the kind of man who went up in balloons those days, and that is how he died.

After that, Etta and I liked to meet in the shade of the bridge, and once when I was not waiting there she came to find me.

That was when she kissed me through the screen door and told me that she liked me.

I wish I knew what ever happened to her. I guess my Father's business did not prosper; and so my Mother took us children out to western Kansas to visit with her father and mother until my Father found a better place for us to live.

I can't remember that we said good-by. It all just vanished in a vast new world, and was a dream.

I went back there to lecture once when I was over sixty. The great stone columns were in place. The bridge still spanned the street. The monument was there, still waiting in its sad forever.

I tried to find someone who, by happy chance, had heard the music of that name.

But there was no one.

6

You cross the Solomon, driving south from Stockton, and it's seven miles from there before you leave the highway and Today. By and by, along the hazy skyrim southeastward—

maybe eighty years away — you see the Twin Buttes, looking like two giant loaves of bread.

It's the same wide, lonely picture you remember from the time when you were five and riding in an old farm wagon out to Grandpa Culler's place. It was so far to anywhere in that strange, endless world of Kansas then, and the creaking wagon only limped along. Or when it tried to hurry, while the horses jogged a bit, it bumped and jerked and jiggled, and you were glad when the horses chose to walk again.

The road by which you leave the highway now runs sharply to the right like any proper, educated road, and has no memories at all. But eighty years ago it strolled southwestward in a desultory fashion across the unfenced prairie until it came at last to Grandpa's homestead in the valley.

Now, two miles onward from the highway, you turn, sharp-cornered, to the left along a road that has not quite forgotten the old days. Then all at once, you're there! It's just across a shallow marshy draw, spanned by a broken culvert, and up a little slope.

The barbed-wire gate is fastened open, surely not to offer a hearty welcome, but rather just because there's so little on the outside wanting in, and nothing on the inside to get out.

I park my car and enter.

No dogs bark.

It's a quiet, never-never, empty place, half enclosed by gnarled box elders. Some ancient cottonwoods that tower along the draw deepen the silence when their high leaves rustle. Across the bottom eastward the tawny short-grass prairie rises to the plain beyond.

They told me it was here. This has to be the place that I came so far, in space and time, to see.

Or is it?

There's some dimension lacking. Surely the miles and turns were counted right. But just how far ago is Yesterday, and where should I have left the road of Now back yonder?

Here Time has gone to sleep and everything is dreaming. Where did those old, neglected box elders ever come from?

12

A little while ago they were not there. And yonder in a patch of weeds a little to the left and towards the draw must be the ruins of the old dug well.

Yes, less some lost dimension, this is it, the very place; and if it's so, a little while ago but far away, I saw my young Grandfather planting whips of cottonwood where now the giants tower in the draw.

This low mound that I'm standing on must be the old sod house gone back to earth—as all the others have who once lived here. Yonder, half a dozen steps to eastward, that weedy, caved-in hole was surely Grandma's cellar. (There was cool, rich buttermilk to drink there after churning.)

And farther on, there in the flat, another and smaller mound would have to be Grandfather's blacksmith shop. That was a place of wonder. Why, with his naked hand, hammer-hardened to the likeness of a hoof, he could scrape the crusted metal from a white-hot iron bar, and never feel it!

Grandpa could make most anything—and did for all the thinly scattered neighbors miles around.

I remember once the way he stroked his long brown beard and told me (with a twinkle in his china-blue eyes, I'm sure), "Yes, yes, boy, I can make anything at all but spotted pigs, and I can make them too without the spots!" I thought it must be so, somehow, because he said it. But maybe he was joking me again.

And sometimes when he drew a red-hot, sparkling bar of iron from the forge, he'd spit a gob of plug tobacco on the anvil, slap the sizzling bar upon it, and hit it with his hammer. When he got this done just right, it sounded almost like a cannon!

And farther yet to eastward where the weeds are tallest now, the straw-roofed barn would be. And that's where Zip was living when I knew her in her prime. She was a pacing mare, doubling as a work horse, and you really should have seen her hitched to a buggy! When my Uncle clucked and touched her with the whip, how she squatted to her job of making tracks and fairly tore the earth up getting yonder!

7

There were no trees about here yet. The two-room house looked out upon a world of grass and sky, save where green corn made careless, extravagant promises on a field to southward.

It was a cozy, homey house, thick-walled against the summer heat and winter cold. The sod, laid up like slabs of stone, but lacking mortar, had come from where the corn was waving yonder—a root-bound grassy ribbon flowing from the mouldboard of a breaking plow to be cut into sections for the builders.

The floor was clay, hard-beaten and foot-polished to the semblance of smooth stone. The ceiling was a sheet of unbleached muslin stretched from wall to wall, partly "for looks," but more to catch the slowly sifting dust. For the roof was made of sod laid out on poles of cottonwood, from somewhere on the Solomon, with clay upon the sod and shale upon the clay for turning water. It was several years after the covered-wagon journey all the way from Indiana and the building of the home before Pa was able to finance this fine improvement and Ma could keep things neater. No doubt it made her positively "throughother" to see things all "glakid" and "clatty" with the dust she was forever chasing. Those are words from Grandma's private vocabulary. She made them by herself to fit her urgent needs for expression; and it may be assumed she used them here. Years later they were current still—especially "throughother," which I think deserves an honored place in Webster.

One room was filled with beds, and there were muslin curtains hung ingeniously to meet the needs of modesty. The cookstove in the other room both fed and warmed the family, getting fuel from the prairie whence the house itself had grown.

It was an all-family project—"picking buffalo chips." We called them "cow chips" later; but the former term might well have been correct, for it was only a matter of a few years since the last of the bison were grazing thereabouts. The still-un-grassed buffalo wallows, scattered here and there, witnessed the fact.

"Picking chips" was happy work for everybody, and we youngsters were proud that we could help almost as much as Grandma and our Mother could. Striking out across the open prairie with a deep-boxed wagon and a co-operative team, we ran about, pulling the sun-dried "pancakes" from the curly grass and sailing them against the wagon's bang-board. It was fun. And it was more, for by wintertime there'd be a reassuring heap of chips against the coming northwest winds and the blizzards. And it was first-rate fuel, burning brightly into coals that glowed and smouldered when you shut the dampers down. Sunflowers too made useful kindling for summer cooking or for starting fires, and they grew big and woody in the draws.

It was a happy place and time, as I remember it; for Hope, too, grew big in Kansas. A little now was much, for next year would be better. The drouth last year was over, and the corn was doing well. Faith and a little rain—that was all the country needed.

Already there was talk around the kitchen table about the new stone house that Grandpa was going to build for Ma. Al-ready he had opened up a limestone quarry on the hillside yonder; and whenever he had some time to spare from his forge, he'd drill and blast some more or dress another stone for Grandma's house.

8

The hotwind came that summer.

The Kansas hotwind is not just a common wind that hap-pens to be hotter than winds usually are. It may better be conceived as a mighty self-completing Presence, a sort of Elemental Being that takes over and destroys.

It came when corn was thriving in the silk—a purring, gentle breathing from the clear southwest at daybreak. By gusty puffs it grew until at noon it boomed—a charging blast that took your breath away.

And it was growing hotter, hotter, hotter.

All night it roared beneath a cloudless sky; and when the white-hot sun glared in upon the tortured world, it was as though a sky-wide furnace door were opened.

Years afterward I wrote about the hotwind in my *The Song of the Messiah*, and it was that summer down in Kansas I remembered:

> The cornstalks, drooping in the bitter dust,
> Despairing mothers widowed in the silk,
> With swaddled babies dead for want of milk,
> Moaned to the wind the universal dearth.

9

And yet it was truly a happy place and time, with everybody neighbors, near or miles apart, and everybody poor but none a pauper. I felt this as a boy, although I couldn't understand it.

Even color did not matter in that humane commonwealth of great need and valiant hope. Our nearest neighbors to the south were Negroes—the Nivens family—the sort of neighbors who share fresh bakings of bread or come to sit up with the sick, maybe bringing a pot of baked beans to help with the cookin'.

When she was very old, my Grandmother was quick to defend the colored people against all comers. "Don't you tell me anything bad about the Negroes," she would say, "for I know too much, so I do; I know too much!" Then she would tell about the time when Pa was so sick and the big snow came.

My Uncle played the fiddle for the square-dance parties around the country, and sometimes he took me with him. I remember well the dancing on the prairie one night when the moon was big and brilliant. I can hear the dancers singing all together with the fiddle:

> Buffalo girls, are you coming out tonight,
>   Coming out tonight, coming out tonight?
> Buffalo girls, are you coming out tonight
>   To dance by the light of the moon?
>
> Yes, O yes, we're coming out tonight,
>   Coming out tonight, coming out tonight.
> Yes, O yes, we're coming out tonight
>   To dance by the light of the moon.

I can hear the monotonously rhythmic fiddle, the pounding of the men's feet, the swishing of the girls' skirts, the laughter, and the high singing voice of the caller—"Swing your pardners, and a do-see-do!" And I can feel something of the lusty joy of it all that stirred me even then without my knowing why.

Then, all of a sudden, the surprised waking in bed at Grandpa's house!

Then there was the "box social," generally held in the schoolhouse, which was the social center of the far-flung neighborhood. It was at once a source of fun and a means of raising money for some local need. Competitive bidding for the boxed lunches that were furnished by the ladies caused great merriment at times, especially when the guarded secret of a box's ownership leaked out, and the bidding became a tough financial battle for a girl, whose heart, it was assumed, went with the box!

Sometimes the "sociable" and the "literary" were united for an evening's entertainment. A "literary" was the country's bow to Culture, as well as a happy way of meeting friendly folks.

A literary program was a triumph of the democratic arts.

17

If you could carry a tune and liked to sing, you sang. If you could fiddle, why you fiddled. If you had some skill in drawing, you could sketch a picture on the blackboard. Or maybe you were clever doing card tricks, so you mystified the people with your skill. If dancing was your strong point, then you danced. Or perhaps you liked the art of speaking pieces, so you spoke one. Young as I was at the time, I still remember someone telling about how he smoked his last cigar, and taking a long time doing it. Also I remember someone aping the clang and clamor of bells—probably Poe's—and I was sorry when someone told how Little Eva died. Even the little children could have a place on the program. I myself, a small bashful towhead, made history one night at the old schoolhouse up the hill a piece from Grandpa's house. I spoke a "poem" my roguish Uncle taught me, and it ran like this:

> As I came down the new-cut road
> I met a possum and a toad;
> And every time the toad would jump,
> The possum bit him on the rump!

That was my first speaking engagement, and I brought down the house. I was so surprised and scared I wet my new pants!

10

That was about the time of the great prairie fire.

I remember how, one day, the horizon to the northeastward was darkened with a cloud that didn't look like rain; and how it grew higher, slowly spreading wider all forenoon.

Some neighbor men came by on horseback, and stopped to talk about the fire off yonder, and how the wind was blowing, and maybe it would change by evening or go down. Then my Uncle saddled Zip, and they all galloped off together and disappeared beyond the hill rim toward the cloud.

When they came riding back, my Grandfather quit his shop, harnessed up a team, and began plowing around and around the straw-roofed barn; and by evening he was turning furrows along the draw where slough grass stood tall and tinder-dry from the recent hotwind.

I remember the tickly feel of danger in the air, the fearful thrill of something big about to happen. I could feel that even Grandfather was afraid, at least a little.

After he came riding back with the neighbor men, my Uncle drove some cows and calves into a barbed-wire enclosure back of the sod house where they would be safe. And there he put the wagon, too, and tied the horses to the wheels. The grownups left us children at the house and told us not to be afraid. Then they went down across the draw and started spreading backfires along the plowing.

Night came down upon us huddled together on the doorstep—a terrifying blackness—the blacker for the lurid luminescence of the rolling smoke yonder and the flaring of the backfires in the slough grass of the draw. I could see the grownups yonder like shadows dancing in and out among the flames as they kept their backfires in control and burning toward the wind by beating them with grain sacks soaked in buckets at the well or in the springy puddles of the slough.

I was five years old, and when the storm of fire broke over the hill rim with its deep voice like thunder sleeping and its blast of flaming day, I started for my Mother with the others yonder in the draw. It seemed the thing of terror was headed straight for me.

A gulch packed full of dried tumbleweeds took fire all at once and exploded in a roaring geyser of sparkling light, leaving a sense of total blackness all about me. I was lost in a nightmare world of burning blindness, until Grandpa picked me up and all of us ran back across the draw.

The plowing and the backfires had made an island of safety for us; but a high wind was blowing, full of sparks at times, and it seemed the barn would surely go. But somehow it didn't. We waited in the suffocating smoke and heat, watching the sky-wide glare of burning night that seemed bending inward, closing slowly on us.

— And then it was morning.

A quarter of a century later I recalled the splendid terror of that night when I wrote the chapter about a prairie fire on the northern plains in my *The Song of Three Friends:*

> . . . he turned and looked and knew
> What birdless dawn, unhallowed by the dew
> Came raging from the Northwest . . .
>
> . . . .
>
> . . . The firm, familiar world,
> It seemed, was melting down, and Chaos swirled
> Once more across the transient realms of form
> To scatter in the primal atom-storm
> The earth's rich dust and potency of dreams.
> Infernal geysers gushed, and sudden streams
> Of rainbow flux went roaring up the skies
> Through ghastly travesties of Paradise,
> Where, drowsy in a tropic summertide,
> Strange gaudy flowers bloomed and aged and died —
> Whole seasons in a moment. Bloody rain,
> Blown slant like April silver, spewed the plain
> To mock the fallow sod; and where it fell
> Anemones and violets of hell
> Foreran the fatal summer.
>
> . . . .
>
> . . . A blinding gloom
> Crushed down; then, followed by a rolling boom,
> There broke a scarlet hurricane of light
> That swept the farthest reaches of the night
> Where unsuspected hills leaped up aghast.
>
> . . . .
>
> And now the wind grew hotter. Overhead
> Inverted seas of color rolled and broke,
> And from the combers of the litten smoke
> A stinging spindrift showered . . .
>
> . . . .

. . . By and by
Drab light came seeping through the sullen sky.
· · · · · · · · · · · · · · · · ·

The wind had died and not a sound arose
Above those blackened leagues; for even crows
(The solitude embodied in a bird)
Had fled that desolation.

11

But that was long before the little house and Ma and Pa
returned to earth—long before Time went to sleep here and
everything fell dreaming.

As I sit here in this place of knowing silence, guarded by
the gnarled box elders and drowsy with the rustle of high
leaves, I close my eyes, and days no longer move, and all the
years exist together. I can see my Grandfather as he was here,
with his long brown beard and bright blue eyes—young and
brisk. And I can see my old Grandmother the way she was
years after Pa was gone, rocking restlessly in her chair. And
I can hear her saying, with the glow of remembered happiness upon her withered face, "Oh, John, if I could only be in
our covered wagon again, going West with Pa and the babies!"

The pile of dressed stone yonder by the long-deserted garden (where delicious "apple-melons" used to grow) is still
waiting for next spring (or is it autumn or the spring thereafter?) when Grandpa will begin to work on Grandma's
house. I saw him forging and tempering the six-toothed chisel
that left his mark of love on every block.

I know the heartachy story of that waiting pile of stone—
how the grasshoppers came, and the hotwinds, and how the
hard years passed; until Hope was no longer enough. So once
more the covered wagon, pulled by Zip and some old harness
friend, set out to find the elusive new home in the West.

In the great sand country of western Nebraska Hope flourished again with the green promises of rainy springs and lucky summers. But the hailstorms came—ironic furies hurling chunks of ice to match the devastations of the hotwind.

Then, by and by, the two were no longer young enough for covered-wagon travel, and, anyway, there were no more Wests.

—And no more babies either.

When I myself was old, I made a pious pilgrimage to the place of that final defeat. It was not easily located, for my Grandparents left no mark upon that far-flung land.

The tax receipts at the County Courthouse furnished the necessary description, and one who specialized in locating lands for oil prospectors led us at last to Grandpa's farm.

My God! My Grandpa's farm!

There are three stunted and discouraged trees, clearly without a future.

There is a hole that must have been a cellar once, but no sign of a house or barn.

There is a decrepit old wagon whose badly weathered wheels, sunk deep in drifted sand, suggest how long ago its last team was unhitched. Could it be the covered wagon, now no longer young enough to travel? I want to think it is.

A battered windmill, leaning crazily out of true, ignores the worrying winds.

There is the melancholy horizon; there is the vast sandy flat.

And nothing else.

A brief description of the place as I saw it may be read in my *The Song of Jed Smith:*

> . . . Level as the sea,
> And like a picture of Eternity
> Completed for the holding of regret.

22

I am back in Kansas now, about to leave the place where everything is dreaming.

This time as I pass through the gate, I close it gently and wire it firmly shut, wondering why I should take the trouble. Surely there is nothing on the inside wanting out, and nothing on the outside wanting in. But it seems, somehow, the way you close the door of a quiet room where someone dear is sleeping and greatly needs the rest.

13

It was Kansas City at last, but hardly the magnificent dream my sisters and I had fancied. We lived awhile in a scary place of bricks at Fourth and Oak, whatever that meant. It was a homesick place. No grass grew there, and strange, unfriendly people who looked dirty lived there too. At night they made loud noises, and sometimes there was fighting.

When we were at Grandpa's out West, Kansas City was a tall beautiful town where wonderful things were always happening, and all the people there were kind and good. We talked and talked about it. We even built a Kansas City out of chips of shale on a jutting ledge overhanging the marshy valley and near to Grandpa's quarry. We spent glorious hours building that City of Happiness where Papa was making a nice home for us, and soon we would go there to live forever and ever.

And now we were there at last!

It is not difficult to understand what had happened: My Father, not very far removed from the backwoods boy he had been, unschooled and unskilled, taking the only job he could find — night watchman at a disreputable "hotel" — and finding temporary shelter for his family nearby.

There is a story in this connection that I must have heard from my Mother years later. I am boyishly proud of it yet, for it makes my Father a hero of sorts. The son of the "hotel" proprietor, having been put out of the house for being drunk and disorderly, had returned sober to settle matters once and for all with the overzealous night watchman. The fight, which I gather was rather Homeric, took place in my Father's room, locked on the inside by the murder-minded invader. I am proud to report that when the police pushed through the assembled audience in the hall and broke down the door, they were barely in time to release the blue-faced intruder and give him back his windpipe!

I can well believe my Father came out on top in that melee, for I have seen him stripped to swim—a V-shaped little giant of a man, five feet five, gaunt-waisted, barrel-chested, and agile as a cat.

We did not live there long. In fact, I don't remember living long in any one place. It may have been the rent that kept us moving.

About here began a timeless Golden Age for us, as I recall it yonder on the far side of Sorrow. It was very brief in fact, but seeming endless in the being, the way one feels about a long, windless summer day. When I judge it by the calendar I'm astonished that it was not half a lifetime at the least.

My Father was making thirty-five dollars a month as conductor on the city cable-car system; and when he worked at night also, helping to repair or replace worn cables, his income must have been impressive! My Mother took in sewing for the neighbors when there were any dresses to make and any free change around to pay for the dresses.

Thus, it will be seen, there was a firm economic basis for our Golden Age.

We had drifted out to Twenty-fifth Street and were stationary awhile. On his one day off a week, my Father and I would escape from civilization, taking to the country and the woods. "Country" began at Thirtieth and Prospect in those days. (That was where our gang stripped naked, walking unimpeded the remainder of the way to our Brush Creek swimming hole.)

When the blessed day of adventure came around, my Mother, having washed and dressed me, would turn me over to my Father. He never said a word about where we were going or what we would do. He just offered his forefinger— I took it, and we went.

Entering the woods, we climbed rail fences, splashed across creeks, and sat down at intervals to rest in green glooms of leafy shade.

Once we came to a deep, clear, shady pool where the creek slept awhile in the heat of the day. Telling me to undress, he went behind a bush. I sat on a rock until he came bounding forth, one shielding hand cupped modestly over his nakedness. Seizing me with his free arm, he waded into the pool and with me across his shoulder swam about on his back, floating like a cork.

He was a silent mystery, full of surprises. Anything might happen with him. Once when I was six or seven we found a hive of wild bees pouring like cold molasses down the side of a tree. Indicating that I was to sit on a log and wait, he disappeared into deep woods. Not a word of explanation! So I waited on my log and was beginning to feel panicky, all alone there in the wilderness, when he returned as silently as he had left with a barrel upon his back. I could not ask him what he was going to do. I never asked questions of my Father. So I watched him from my log and saw him build a smudgy fire under the swarm, which he then swept into the barrel. Without a word he shouldered the barrel and took off for home with me at his heels.

The bees were added to our back-yard menagerie, which included two squirrels, a whippoorwill that we had found with a broken wing, a big, savage, solemn horned owl, a coon, and a tubful of crawdads (for the coon). The swarm soon left us, to resume an interrupted ecstasy, I suppose, for it was springtime.

And once when we were wandering in the woods we came

suddenly into a small circular clearing full of sunlight and silence. And in the center thereof a single wild crab-apple tree was blooming gloriously. I remember how we stood still there for quite a while, just looking. It seemed we were having an adventure somehow. I wish my Father had told me what he was thinking about the tree busily making beauty there in a lonely place. I'd love to quote him here.

14

But if that was an adventure, what of the time we went to visit the Missouri in flood! We were standing on a blufftop in Kansas City, and the whole world beneath us, and far as we could see, was a chaos of wild waters. It was my second encounter with elemental grandeur; and what happened to me that day as I stood on the windy blufftop, holding fast to my Father's forefinger for safety, did much to determine the direction of my lifelong striving. Many years later, when I had descended the river in my own boat from the head of navigation at Fort Benton, I recorded in my *The River and I* something of my experience that day:

. . . the summer had smitten the distant mountains, and the June floods ran. Far across the yellow swirl that spread out into the wooded bottom-lands, we watched the demolition of a little town. The siege had reached the proper stage for a sally, and the attacking forces were howling over the walls. The sacking was in progress. Shacks, stores, outhouses, suddenly developed a frantic urge to go to St. Louis. It was a weird retreat in very bad order. A cottage with a giant window that glared like the eye of a Cyclops, trembled, rocked with the athletic lift of the flood, made a panicky plunge into a convenient tree; groaned, dodged, and took off through the brush like a scared cottontail. . . . This daredevil boy-god that sauntered along with a town in its pocket, and a steepled church under its arm for a moment's toy! . . .

. . . But the first sight of the Missouri River was not enough for

26

me. There was a dreadful fascination about it—the fascination of all huge and irresistible things. I had caught my first wee glimpse into the infinite; I was six years old.

Many a lazy Sunday stroll took us back to the river; and little by little the dread became less, and the wonder grew—and a little love crept in.

It was not without good reason that a friendly critic, commenting on *The River and I*, referred to "that very natural love affair between Neihardt and the River."

15

I am on Vine Street in Kansas City, and how I got here I do not know, for I have no memory of moving to this place—perhaps because there was so very little to move. It is an ugly neighborhood, and utterly lacking in boys to play with, it seems to me. Up Vine a block or more and eighty years ago sits Bryant School, looking dourly virtuous and coldly unrelenting. Nearby is a gas well in the middle of the street. It was burning with a windy flare a good long lifetime ago, and should be burning yet in this weird backwash of time.

The wooden sidewalk here spans a tiny spring creek that manages to survive in a lingering dream of vanished woodlands. There is a railing on the span, and one leaning on it gazing down sees a clear little pool with minnows busy being happy in it. There is a thin sheet of ice on the pool now, for it is late autumn, and this has added a touch of mystery to the crystal depths.

Familiar with great waters as I am since the discovery of the flooding Missouri, I can make the pool as big as I like just by staring hard at it awhile and imagining. If I think myself very tiny, the pool can become a vast sea, haunted by huge savage whales and hungry for little ships.

This little bridge has become my means of escape from

loneliness in an ugly neighborhood without boys. I can come here any time, look down a little while, and see!

I was doing this one day when a nice man with a clock under one arm tapped me on my head, and when I looked up, he smiled and asked me if I lived around here. I did; and he said: "Do you folks have a clock?" and we didn't; so he said: "I wish you would take me to see your mother. I want to show her my clock." And I said if he wanted money for his clock we didn't have any. And he said he didn't want hardly any money at all, and he was sure my Mother would like his clock. So I took him to see my Mother.

She was sewing in the back room where we lived. Our front door was in the alley, and in the other room between us and the street were strangers who talked loud so that we heard most everything they said.

My Mother did like the clock, and so did my sisters. Who wouldn't? It stood about two feet high, with fancy scrollwork all around its face, which gleamed with polished brass. (I know this, because that clock lived with us until all of us were old.) The man made it do things. He turned the hands and it knew exactly when to bong for the hours and half-hours!

My Mother put her name to a paper, promising to pay money! It was a rash thing to do; but we all liked the clock so much, and surely there'd be a way to find twenty-five cents every month when the nice man came around to collect.

I do believe that was the beginning of a better life for all of us, though we didn't know it then. It seemed to raise us to a higher social level, and its faithful, confident account of the busy hours made us feel livingly a part of the great world. Bong! Bong! Bong!

It did us a special service that winter, too. As Christmastime approached, we made much of our family clock as a present for all of us to share. How could one expect more? Bong!

But my sisters had heard at school that the Kansas City Christmas Wagon would come around on Christmas Eve with presents for children. And so on Christmas Eve we all sat up waiting for the wagon—all except my Father, who was working all night with the streetcar cables downtown. It was a long sleepy wait; but by and by there was a jingling of sleigh bells out in front and merry talk in the room where the strangers lived. Then someone said: "Is there anybody else living here?" And someone answered: "There's nobody else living here—just us. Merry Christmas! Merry Christmas!" Then the happy little sleigh bells began jingling again and died away.

I think we would have cried if our clock had not come awake just then, bonging bravely and often!

After all, how many people had a Christmas present like that?

16

It was in the Early Clock period of our domestic history that my formal education began. It didn't last very long at first. In fact, it was practically instantaneous, as will be seen.

My sisters, two and four years older than I, had been in school for some time; and as I was now eight years old, it seemed high time for me to surrender my freedom, put on shoes, and begin to realize that "life is real and life is earnest."

So one morning my Mother took me to Bryant School and turned me over to a man who appeared unnaturally tall and large. Also, as I recall it now, he had an authoritative voice that scared me.

I remember how seriously scrubbed and polished I was, how stiffly starched my shirt felt, and how conspicuous my new pants seemed! I was ashamed of them for their offensive newness, and for the damning fact that they did not come from a store! Surely, I thought, anyone could see that my Mother had made them!

The tall man asked questions of my Mother and put the answers in a book. Then he said she could go, and I could wait. He put me in a little room nearby and said he would be back.

I sat and waited. No one came. The mingled yells, shouts, howls, and screams of the playground increased alarmingly; and suddenly, gripped by a green sick panic, I broke jail! No one noticed me stealing into the big empty room and out onto the front stone steps. Then I took out at top speed and I did not stop until I reached the bridge over my vast little sea, full of whales and hungry for ships.

That was it! "And the morning and the evening were the first day."

I think we must have moved again about that time, for I never went back to Bryant.

17

Thus my first encounter with Education ended in a wild retreat, as here shamelessly related. But soon thereafter I found Dick Scammon, and that made all the difference.

We had recently moved to Park Avenue near Twenty-fifth. A little more than a block away on Brooklyn stood the home of Judge Scammon, a huge three-story mansion, as I remember it, set in a spacious lawn. I think it had been a country estate with extensive landscaped grounds before the city had invaded the region; but, if so, it was still a noble reminder of more gracious and leisurely times.

Sometimes stylish carriages drawn by sleek horses in shiny harness stopped there; and almost any afternoon nice-looking people were to be seen playing tennis, or sitting on the wide porch laughing and talking.

It was a strange, fascinating world to me, and I liked to sit under a tree on the opposite side of the street, observing the manners and customs of that alien world where everyone, young and old, was happy—and rich, too, or how else could they be so happy?

I was especially interested in a boy of about my age—

though he was taller—who often romped roughly with the biggest dog I had ever seen. It didn't seem possible that I could ever know the boy, he was so far away in his superior world. To put it simply, it was easy to see that he was "rich people."

But one day a miracle happened. The boy actually came running with his dog to where I was sitting under my tree.

I had never known a boy like him. Sometimes he talked like a grownup or like something out of a book, and he was very polite.

I will try to reconstruct our first meeting as best I can after eighty years.

"Pardon me, sir," he said, holding out his hand, which I took eagerly, "but my name is Dick. What is yours, please?" I told him it was John. He said, "That is a fine old name. I prefer it to my own."

Patting the dog on his head, he said: "This gentleman is a Saint Bernard, and his name is Plato. He understands, but cannot speak, English—only Greek. Plato, you will recall, was a great Greek philosopher."

I didn't recall, but I *was* impressed.

Placing a hand on the dog's head, he said: "Kindly sit up, Plato, and shake hands with our new friend." The dog obeyed, politely bored.

"What do you like to play?" he asked.

I said I liked playing cable cars because my father was a conductor.

"Oh, that must be most interesting," he exclaimed. "We will have to play that sometime soon. My father is a judge, but one can't play that very well.

"Are you by any chance interested in the Trojan War?"

I had not yet heard that hostilities had broken out, and I lamely admitted as much.

"It's not really happening now, you know, the way *common* things do," he said. "It's a story that will live forever, my mother says, and so it will always be happening. Come on and I'll show you."

So he and Plato and I trotted off across the street, over the soft wide lawn, and past the huge house to the stable.

A stairway led to a large room off the haymow. It was Dick's treasure house; and there I had my first glimpse of Homer's world.

The walls of the place were covered with pictures of warriors in chariots, gods and goddesses, kings and heroes. It is probable that some of the large posters had been made for the Priests of Pallas parade.

"This is Zeus," said Dick, pointing to a heavily whiskered, sour-faced old codger sitting on a cloud with a fistful of lightning.

"And that is Achilles dragging Hector; and there you see Troy burning, all because of Helen, they say; but I don't believe it. Do you? She was much more beautiful than any picture can make her look, you know, and so you see there is no picture of her here."

It was all most exciting and bewildering, and several visits to the treasure room were required to clarify some points. For instance, I had supposed a chariot was a *troj* used in war and that every hero went to war in a *troj*, hence *Troj in War*. When Dick explained my error, he didn't laugh. Anyone could make that mistake, he said, and a chariot *did* look the way *troj* sounds. That was like Dick.

One day he took me to see his mother, a sweet, gracious lady who liked boys. She spent the forenoons in her study, writing stories, Dick said; some of them for *The Youth's Companion,* using her maiden name, Laura Everingham, for a pen name. But in the afternoons she was free, and we spent many golden hours listening to the stories she told of "old, unhappy, far-off things and battles long ago." I think I heard most of the *Iliad* and *Odyssey* from her; and how she could make a story come alive!

Sometimes the Judge himself would invite us into the great, silent library, where he read to us with illuminating comments. He was tall and big and dignified. The first time I heard about Jove, I was struck by the resemblance! I remember especially how he read *Rasselas* to us and made it seem really exciting with his running commentary.

As I recall my association with Dick, it seems we must have been together for years; but it could not have been more than a matter of months.

How much I was influenced by my experiences in that enchanted world, I can only guess. It was not until I had passed out of boyhood that they came to seem more than a way of playing peculiar to Dick.

18

My next memory of school is a happy one on the whole. Also, we were living in a real house on Wabash near Howard, where we had good friends. For a while before that, we lived at 2428 Olive Street; and it was then, I suppose, that I resumed my interrupted educational career at Irving School. I must have seemed well advanced when I began, for I remember that I could read a whole baking-powder can with ease and do considerable sums, if they were not too considerable.

My progress was rapid and before long I was in the fourth grade.

But here it must be clearly understood that I had a goddess for a teacher! Her name was Miss Lulu Lobb. Oh, I know what you are thinking—that no goddess ever had a name like that. I myself was unprepared to believe it—until I saw—and you too shall see.

I want to give my reader-friends a faithful account of this affair, realizing, however, that an old man and a boy are inextricably mixed in the teller.

I will begin by attempting a factual description of the divine lady—insofar as such may be possible.

Miss Lobb was tall and slender, with a mass of pale-gold hair piled high in coils on the top of her head. Her eyes were gray-blue. I suppose her complexion might be described as milk-white. Her voice was low and gentle. Her mode of loco-motion was especially notable; she did not walk, she glided — partly, no doubt, because of her natural grace and partly because skirts fell well below the ankle in those days of inno-cence.

At that time boys and girls were required to be seatmates, in keeping with a current theory that each would exert a fine moral and spiritual influence on the other.

It was a noble experiment.

My seatmate, I regret to recall, was a wicked little girl by the name of Lily. She had a retroussé nose, liberally freckled, and a hearty scorn for all boys as a nation of people. Lily was undeniably clever, and occasionally she would plague me by making offensive noises that seemed to emanate from my half of the seat. Thereupon she would regard me shrinkingly, as from an insufficient distance, staging a show of sensitive innocence worthy of her name.

At this critical moment in my history, I was engaged in the manufacture of an "apple-faker." This was an ingenious in-strument designed to aid in the borrowing of apples from the huckster's wagon with minimum risk. It consisted of a cork with a horseshoe nail thrust through it endwise and a straight feather affixed in the nail hole at the top. A twine string was fastened to the nailhead for recovery of the instrument when thrown into a pile of apples — with one impaled thereon, it was hoped. I was proud of my apple-faker, which I weighted with lead for better casting. Some of the more heroic boys of my acquaintance reported brilliant success in using my faker, but I was far more interested in making a really good faker than in using it when made.

On this fateful afternoon, I had a spare horseshoe nail in my pocket; and when Lily furtively went into action against me, I did an ungentlemanly thing. Ignoring all moral and spiritual influences, if any, I vigorously pricked her leg with the keen point of my nail.

Lily had an enormous voice packed away in her apparently

34

frail body, and she turned it on all at once, together with her high-capacity fountain of tears.

During the excitement I was hustled into the cloakroom, there to await punishment after school.

It was a warm autumn afternoon, and when at last I heard my roommates bustling into line for the march out, I was grateful that no one had worn coats or overshoes that day, so that no one might see me there in my disgrace.

The drums began and the sound of many marching feet arose and rolled down the broad stairs and out of the rooms, across the big central hall, breaking into shouts of freedom as the leaders of the columns reached the outside doors and bolted.

I waited, feeling something like the approach of doom in the slow ebb of sound as the marchers decreased. At last the drums ceased. The "tumult and the shouting" died away into a bodeful silence.

Then all at once I knew that she was there above me!

I did not look up, but I remember her low, soft voice: "You have always been such a good boy until now, and I am sorry I must punish you for what you did. Hold out your hand, please."

(*Please*, to *me*, the most miserable of mortals!)

I did hold out my hand, and she took it in her long, white fingers, bending back the palm, which she began spatting with a ruler.

I was surprised that she did not spat hard at all, and pretty soon I looked into her face away up there in heaven — and I saw!

I saw the most beautiful thing I had ever seen! I saw a real goddess smiling down on me and *her eyes were all wet.*

She wasn't spatting my hand any more, and I wished she would go on. But she just looked down at me with her face shining and her eyes wet. So I wasn't afraid at all, and I said: "Honest, I didn't make that bad noise; but I'm awful sorry for what I did."

35

She stooped and held me close to her for a while; and then she kissed me on the forehead, and let me go.

19

The foregoing is the first installment of a love story "to be continued in our next" and thence to cross the gap of half a century. Much of it must remain untold, for even I, a principal character in the tale, know it largely as dream and inference; and if, by cheating a bit, an overcurious reader should strive to know "how it all comes out," he will arrive at mystery and wonder for his pains.

Our life in Kansas City ended the next spring (1891) and thereafter I was living in a new world of "strange faces, other minds." There was no one around who had ever heard of Miss Lobb, and my memory of her grew dimmer or at least less active. I was ten years old, and there were great dreams to dream, and great things to be done, and tomorrow was a magic word. There must have been years when the name occurred to me in the most casual manner, if at all.

Then one day in school, I caught up with Tennyson's *Dream of Fair Women*. Suddenly there she was, as vividly beautiful as when I saw her last, in the cloakroom looking down at me with wet eyes.

> At length I saw a lady within call
> As still as chiseled marble standing there,
> A daughter of the gods, divinely tall
> And oh, divinely fair!

And later still, when I was in my early teens, reading *The Aeneid* at sight, just for the glory of God and the heady joy of it, I came upon that line where Aphrodite is moving away from her mortal son. According to the text, "She was manifest a goddess by her gait"; and again I felt the thrilling shock of recognition. It was Miss Lobb! There could be no mistaking it!

More years passed by, and I was with Harry Richmond, sick-abed with a high fever, when his teacher came to see him. "She swayed above me," Harry recalls, "like a green tree in the wind and rain."

Maybe it wasn't a goddess Harry saw; but it came upon me with a clutch at the heart that there was something divinely precious he and I both knew!

At the age of twelve the direction of my life changed abruptly. Up to that time it had been taken for granted that I was going to be an inventor. Then I began to write verse; and that is another mystery story I shall want to tell later.

20

By the time I was fifteen years old, I had written three fantastic tales in rather respectable blank verse—*Chalboa*, *Tlingilla*, and *The Wizard of the Wind*. These were given reverently to the flames in 1896 when I began working on *The Divine Enchantment*—a long poem done in various verse forms, and based upon Vedanta thought. This was my first book, published in 1900 by James T. White & Co. of New York. An edition of five hundred was printed. Within a year thereafter I burned all but a score of the edition, keeping the kitchen stove in fuel for weeks.

It was not that I thought ill of the forlorn little book; and several polite reviewers had treated it with respect, just as though the author were a regular man with whiskers! I alone knew what the little book was meant to be, and *was* in part. I alone knew how much it had cost me. And oh, the times when the heavens opened and I *knew* beyond all saying and singing!

—And to think of all those alien, cold, uncaring eyes out yonder in the world! Perhaps something like jealous love prompted the act of destruction.

Seven years later my sequence of love poems, *A Bundle of Myrrh,* was published in New York by the old Outing Publishing Company. The manuscript had been circulating among the clubs of the city for some months before it found a home. "When poetry comes in the front door of this establishment," wrote the president of the firm, "the entire office force goes out the back door; but we can't reject this manuscript." The book made a sensation. By the standards of those innocent days it was regarded, on the whole, as more than a bit "daring"—even shocking in spots. (But was it not a flirtation with delicious sin to view a feminine ankle on a gusty day?) This little book, in fact, was the naïvely reverent record of some exploratory adventures in living experienced by a young man much in love with life—*and* certain glorified ladies! It led the reader quite naturally to another little book, *The Stranger at the Gate,* which was all about the coming of the babies.

Although the *Bundle* covered my developing romantic life for more than a decade and a half, there is nothing in it even remotely reminiscent of my goddess teacher in the cloakroom revelation. Apparently that tale had gone the way of boyhood, to be told no more forever.

But even then a new installment was in preparation. My Mona had just returned from Paris, studying sculpture under the guidance of Auguste Rodin, when *A Bundle of Myrrh* appeared in New York. She was one of many who wrote me enthusiastic letters of appreciation; but she proved to be *the one.* The divine lightning struck. I had the marriage license in my pocket twenty-four hours before I ever saw her with my eyes!

And for almost fifty years thereafter *A Bundle of Myrrh* continued to pay through her comradeship such rich royalties as no publisher's contract ever offered.

21

It must seem that our continued story has ceased to continue; but that is an error. Somehow, somewhere, all the while it must have been telling itself to the silence of the years, for soon now we shall hear it again.

In 1912, at the age of thirty-one, my lyric period ended, and I began the chief work of my life, *A Cycle of the West*. It covers the epic period of the trans-Missouri country, beginning in 1822 and ending in 1890 with the Battle of Wounded Knee, when Indian resistance ended on the Great Plains.

In 1941 the great task was completed, and much of a life-dominating dream had been realized. I was sixty years old — approaching old age, it seemed then; and while I was grateful for the many precious golden years I had been able to give to the task, there was a backlash of sadness in the moment of victory.

At this point it is important to note that at least half a century has passed in our chronology since there has been any reference to my teacher at Irving; and during our thirty-three years of married life I had never had occasion to speak of her to Mona. It was all so far back in my past, which had nothing in common with Mona's memories of an early European childhood.

It was within a week after the last line of the *Cycle* had been written. There had been no talk of it that evening, and we had gone to bed.

I was still wide awake when Mona, evidently dreaming, began to talk with a halting, fuzzy voice.

"But — John — Lulu isn't tall!"

"Of course not!" I said. (My sister Lulu was a little woman.)

"But *this* one is *tall,* and she says her name is Lulu!"

"What in the world are you talking about?" I said.

Then she wakened enough to speak in a nearly normal fashion. A tall, beautiful woman, apparently in her middle twenties, had just come out of the dark, her arms held wide, her face glowing with happiness. "She hugged me," Mona said, "as though sharing some great joy with me. 'I am Lulu,' she said; and standing at her full height, she moved her head slowly from side to side, as though drawing attention to her mass of golden hair, piled high on her head in the Charles Dana Gibson fashion. Then she pointed, smiling; and I looked and saw a white-headed little boy, sitting on his crossed legs off yonder. After a while the light about her began to fade. She turned and slowly moved away into the dark, seeming to glide rather than to walk."

"My God, Mona!" I exclaimed. "That was Miss Lobb, and I must have been the little boy!"

"And who is Miss Lobb?" she asked.

It is a curious fact that I never thought of my teacher as *Lulu*. The name seemed to me offensively inappropriate for a goddess, and I know it only because I saw it on my report card.

This is a true story, honestly told.

Well—?

22

I have followed my goddess across half a century; and, according to our conventional notion of one-way time, I am stalled with my story in the year 1941 at the age of sixty! And it would seem that I have no means of escape except by getting older and older. But that will not do, for I have much unfinished business in the enchanted age from ten to twelve years old, and I must return.

Fortunately, remembering is a dreamlike operation, and in a dream there is no irreversible flow, but a free and unlimited choice of directions.

So I have returned from being sixty years old awhile in

the year 1941, and am ten years old again in the world-changing year of 1891.

Some time ago I recalled our family Golden Age—which followed the Early Clock period—when my Father was drawing thirty-five dollars every month with occasional overtime, and my Mother was making her cool ten cents an hour for dressmaking. It was a peaceful time of plenty and we were living in a nice little cottage at Wabash and Howard. My Father and Mother were like old friends together, so that we children lost the dread of something bad about to happen that we often felt when there was mysterious trouble in the house.

Thanks largely to my Mother, I suspect, we were apparently on the way up, as witnessed by the fact that my older sister, Lulu, was studying painting, and the younger, Grace, was taking both piano and elocution lessons, in preparation for an acting career. Since it was already assumed that I would be a great inventor, no special preparation was needed in my case.

My Father even took us on a glorious steamboat excursion from Kansas City to Leavenworth and return. Until then my longest steamboat voyage was made aboard the grand old ferry *Annie Cade* on one of her numberless crossings from the foot of Main Street. (Does anyone remember the *Annie Cade?*) She must have "found the harbor ways that know the ships of all the sagas, long ago." The Leavenworth trip, by comparison, was almost an ocean voyage.

We had set sail in the morning, but the river was at a very low stage, and the night was getting old before we neared Kansas City on the return trip. Often there was the shivery feel of mysterious hazards being faced when drowsy and troubled passengers grouped about the foredeck, listening to the singsong reading of the river depths by a crewman sounding with the lead. Now and then with a frightened jangling of bells the engines reversed, and she backed out of danger, nosing about for another try, with the searchlight boring into the dark ahead.

My Father told us he had to be at the carbarn by four o'clock in the morning. Our boat had stopped close to the north bank somewhere above the bridge, her stern wheel idly churning the current and her engines snoring peacefully. They seemed sound asleep and enjoying the rest. Everybody was eager to get home and everybody was asking everybody else why we didn't move, but nobody knew.

So my Father told us he couldn't wait and we would have to go on without him. With a running jump he cleared the deck rail and disappeared in the black night. But presently we heard him call back "Good-by."

I suppose he landed on solid ground; but at any rate, he was at the barn by four o'clock, and we reached home at dawn, weary, but glorified by a great experience.

Truly it was our Golden Age, but even then it was ending. I don't know what brought it to a tragic close. Perhaps the fabulous dual income fizzled out. Maybe the streetcar company could not afford to pay such extravagant salaries. Or maybe my Father had thought of a sure-fire investment that would make much more money in a more exciting way. I don't know. But I remember yet, with a twinge of heartache, the angry, terrifying voices that hurt me deep in the middle of my breast.

There was a time when my Father did not come home for several days. Then there was a knocking on the locked door in the night and a low voice called, "Alice." There was no reply. Again the knocking and the voice; but no reply. And after a long silence outside, there was the sound of footsteps going away.

I lay listening to the pounding of my heart and the footsteps until there was only the pounding. Then I had to get up and run to the door and unlock it. The night was black outside and still.

I called, "Good-by, good-by!" — And his voice came back, like a dimming echo.

23

A voice lost in the night! What an ending for a Golden Age! But wise men have said that all is but a beginning; and so it was with us. Soon we were off on the railroad cars for a long weary ride to a wonderful place called Wayne, Nebraska. There my Mother's brother, Uncle George, was farming and my Grandparents had come to rest after their pioneering.

I remember little of the railway journey, except that once in the queer, troubled night the screaming engine scared me wide awake, and I lay listening to the long-drawn, heart-achy wail out yonder in the dark — *G-o-o-d-by-ee, g-o-o-d-by-ee for-ev-er-r-r!*

It was good to be at Grandpa's place once more and to experience again the heavenly *Grandma feeling*. Zip, the blooded pacing mare, was there too. I had loved and petted her when she was a filly in Kansas, and we were like "boys and girls together" down on the old homestead. She seemed to like the kiss I planted on her pretty nose — just like old times. She had shared the family fortunes ever since she first looked through a bridle. And here she was, as pretty as ever, doing her duty like the true aristocrat she was, after the long retreat from hail and hotwinds to this new land of hope.

So the voice from the dark grew dim for a while, and no one ever mentioned my Father. But sometimes it all came back with the ache in my throat of tears too big for crying. Then I would go out into the cornfield — deep into its green, whispering solitude, where no one could see me. And there I would remember and remember. Maybe I recalled the way we got a coon for my back-yard menagerie. That time my Father and I were walking together down Wabash, and I was holding fast to his forefinger, as usual. A Negro came by, leading a coon by a chain, and oh, how I did wish I could have it for a pet! I could not tell my Father as much, but I kept on dragging my feet and looking back yonder where my last hope was about to vanish. Then, without question or comment, he told me to wait right there. I saw him overtake the colored man; and after what seemed to be a stiff argument, my Father came trotting back and handed me the chain with the coon at the end of it!

Or maybe I recalled the time when Grover Cleveland appeared on a second-story balcony of the old Flatiron Building at the junction of Main, Ninth, and Delaware. The crowd was so packed in the five converging streets that a short person might die for lack of breath down under in that crush of bodies. So my Father stood me on his shoulders with his head in my crotch.

When the Great Man appeared up yonder, the shouting crowd surged and swayed so wildly that I lost my Father's head and hat. Whereupon I started out in a panic hunt for them, walking roughshod from shoulder to shoulder, and making havoc among the startled flocks of hats! There was some cussing down there around my ankles until my Father managed to reclaim me somehow!

Or maybe I recalled the time we heard gray old Confederate General Buckner speak (was it at the old Gillis Theater?) about the War Between the States; and how once he wiped his eyes with a big handkerchief and sounded as though he were crying down inside of him. I could remember what he said: "I will never allow the flag of my country to trail in the dust"; but I didn't know why he said it. I felt sorry that a nice old grandpa should feel like that.

24

Very soon we began living in a nice little house in Wayne, where my Mother could get dressmaking to do. She had a special gift for sewing—for *creative* sewing, let us say. She could fashion a beautiful new dress out of an old one—if it wasn't too old; and what couldn't she do with plenty of nice new material! I've heard it said that there was *style* in everything she made. So it was no trouble at all to get a dollar for a ten-hour day. Sometimes she went out to sew at people's homes, and then, in addition to the dollar, she had her dinner free!

I like to think of her as she was in her heyday, plying her magic arts—a pretty little woman with a mouthful of pins, fitting paper patterns to the ample curves of some half-clad lady!

As for me, I was going to be an inventor; and already I had secretly begun my career.

There was a little red book, simply entitled *Electricity*. Where it came from I do not know. As I remember, it wasn't there, and then it *was*. But what a book! A man by the name of Poyser wrote it; and he knew all about Leyden jars and static machines. I thought he must be a very great man, and I regarded his little red book with reverential awe. My Mother helped me to read it with some understanding, and as a result of its teaching I devised a scheme for replacing the big clumsy steel grips on cable cars with magnetic grips operated by batteries. No gripman would be needed to operate my device. The conductor, going about his usual business, had only to press a button conveniently placed, and the invisible magnetic grip would close upon the moving cable down below in the conduit. My Father, as I have noted, had been a cable-car conductor, and I thought he would have been pleased with my invention. Also perhaps he would have been given more money because he could be two men at once—a conductor and a gripman!

Unfortunately, however, cable cars were already going out of fashion. But my improved cable grip was, after all, merely one of my minor inventions. So also was my flying airship, which *almost* flew. All I needed was a light source of power. Even the Wright brothers needed that! Lacking such a source, I even tried to use gravity, there being so much of it around. This was my small contribution to the Flying Age, which had not yet begun; and I believe the Wright brothers were still grounded and would remain so for about ten years.

My major invention, of which I am still boyishly proud, was properly mothered by Necessity. And thus it came about: my pal Frank Whitney and I had built two fleets of toy warships complete with sails rigged in accordance with specific instructions at the back of Webster's *Dictionary*. The flagship of my fleet was the *Constitution*, and Frank's was the *Guerrière*. These honest-to-goodness warships were armed with from two to six cannons made of ten-guage brass shotgun shells. These were furnished with touchholes, and sticks of smouldering punk were used for firing. Our battles took place in convenient ponds near town; these being regarded as seas, if not oceans.

Having loaded all guns with black powder and pebbles and cast lots for the privilege of attacking first, we deployed the fleets in opposing battle lines. Flags arose gloriously to the mastheads; the terrible action began, the attackers firing at will until the last gun was empty.

Then the heroic defense of the battered flotilla began — nor ceased until the last gun had belched defiance at the nefarious foe:

Hurrah for Liberty!

Don't give up the ship!

We have only begun to fight!

Damn the torpedoes!

The fleet that suffered the greater damage was pronounced defeated. Sometimes the destruction was fearful, necessitating a complete overhaul of complex sail systems.

After several campaigns on various seas and oceans of the neighborhood, I grew weary of sailing ships as fighting craft. How exciting it would be to ram the enemy under power after pounding the daylights out of him with cannon fire!

Plainly I needed steam the worst way! But the reciprocating engine was the only type I knew, and how could I ever hope to make it?

I thought and thought. Then at last I had it! I would use a

baking-powder can for a boiler. A lamp wick in a dish of lard would furnish heat. Near the top of the boiler there would be an opening into a cone-shaped cylinder, the small end near the boiler. Inside this there would be a horizontal turning shaft, bearing fan blades of graduated lengths increasing regularly from the boiler outward, thus equalizing the power of the decreasing steam pressure throughout the length of the shaft, which would have to whirl! No two ways about it — that shaft would whirl!

And there you had a steam engine, wholly unlike any known to me or to anyone else so far as I was aware. The whirling shaft could easily be hitched to a propeller at the rear of the craft. And lo — a steamship!

I came very near getting this engine made. All I needed was fifty cents to pay a tinner for some soldering.

This was in 1892. I did not hear of the turbine steam engine until years later, after I had deserted Science for Poetry.

And that is a story I shall tell next.

25

It happened when I was eleven years old, in the fall of 1892. I had just retired from the rugged life of a fighting sea captain to devote all my energies to the development of my engine and the subsequent building of a steamship.

There was hope that the needed capital might still be raised, either by floating a loan or finding a job. But the money market was tight in the nineties, and no one, as yet, had required my services. If I had been willing to divulge my secret, the tinner might have been induced to waive immediate payment, but the fear of ridicule restrained me. And how could I prove that my purpose was not to engage in sinful life or riotous living with that fifty cents?

This was the state of affairs when, one afternoon, I fell

ill. It came upon me suddenly and with little or no warning. The world tottered and began to rotate. Then there was blackness.

When I came to, I was in bed, floating dizzily; and my Mother, grotesquely distorted above me, was holding something cold and wet on my forehead. I tried to speak to her, but she became someone I did not know and slowly dissolved.

Then I was flying face downward, with arms and hands thrust forward like a diver's. There was vastness—terribly empty, save for a few lost stars, too dim and wearily remote ever to be reached. And there was dreadful speed, a speed so great that whatever lay beneath me—whether air or ether—turned hard and slick as glass.

I wanted to rest. I wanted to go home. But when I cried out in desperation, it seemed a great Voice filled the hollow vastness and drove me on. There was something dear to leave behind, something yonder to be overtaken. Faster! faster! faster!

Three times the dream recurred; and in the feverish intervals I held fast to my Mother, fearing to be alone again out there.

When I wakened in the morning, the world was still and the fever was gone.

The foregoing is offered as the dynamic pattern of a dream that changed the direction of my life, and gave me the drive to do. At first it seemed only a curious nightmare. Then it began to take on the mood of sublimity, with less of fear and more of wonder. But it was not until eighteen years later that I felt moved to realize as poetry the mood and meaning of the subconsciously developed dream; and I did so in my lyric, "The Ghostly Brother." I suggest that it be read in the light of what is written here.

It will be noted that there are two contending forces, which may be variously interpreted as expressing the higher and lower conceptions of being; the simple satisfactions of common sense and the costly rewards of spiritual striving; the urgent obligation to give oneself away, to be lost in something

48

impersonal and bigger than oneself; the conception of living as a process of progressive weaning.

.   .   .   .

Brother, Brother, break the gyves!
Burst the prison, Son of Power!
Product of forgotten lives,
Seedling of the final flower!
What to you are nights and days,
Drifting snow or rainy flaw,
Love or hate or blame or praise —
Heir unto the Outer Awe?

I am breathless from the flight
Through the speed-cleft, awful night!
Panting, let me rest awhile
In this pleasant aether-isle.
Here, content with transient things,
How the witless dweller sings,
Rears his brood and steers his plow,
Nursing at the breasts of Now!
Here the meanest, yea, the slave
Claims the heirloom of a grave!
O, this little world is blest —
Brother, Brother, let me rest!

I am you and you are I!
When the world is cherished most,
You shall hear my haunting cry,
See me rising like a ghost.
I am all that you have been,
Are not now, but soon shall be!
Thralled awhile by dust and din —
Brother, Brother, follow me!

'Tis a lonesome, endless quest;
I am weary; I would rest.
Though I seek to fly from you,
Like a shadow, you pursue.

49

Do I conquer? You are there,
Claiming half the victor's share.

. . . .

In the sighing of the rain,
Your voice goads me like a pain.
Happy in a narrow trust,
Let me serve the lesser will
One brief hour—and then, to dust!
O, the dead are very still!

Brother, Brother, follow hence!
Ours the wild, unflagging speed!
Through the outer walls of sense,
Follow, follow where I lead!
Love and hate and grief and fear—
'Tis the geocentric dream!
Only shadows linger here,
Cast by the eternal Gleam!
Follow, follow, follow fast!—
Somewhere out of Time and Place,
You shall lift the veil at last,
You shall look upon my face;

. . . .

26

———◇———

"The Ghostly Brother," quoted above, was written at about
the age of thirty, near the end of my lyric-writing period. The
dream with which it is concerned came when I was turning
twelve. Looking back over my work of the intervening years,
I note the influence of the dream in single lines, in passages,
or in whole poems, as well as in an overall sense of urgent obligation that such reminiscent passages recall. Traces of the
dream are to be found even in *A Cycle of the West*—notably in

The Song of Hugh Glass, written twenty years after the dream. At the same time, it is to be noted, the dream itself was developing unconsciously.

The five years following the dream, 1893 to 1898, were so crowded with activities and achievements that it is difficult to review them in a single story. First of all, there were at least two of me contending for the role of protagonist. For instance, while one of me was living a carefree and exciting Tom Sawyer life with my pal John Chaffee, there was another one of me secretly concerned with leaving behind him, at his early death, some worthy work that might compensate for the potatoes he had eaten and the roofs that had protected him! This seems funny enough at the age of more than ninety years, but at the time it was profoundly sincere, as will be seen later in this history.

So I will begin with the story of my continuing education, holding the concurrent story of another me for subsequent telling.

27

According to my report card (signed by Lulu Lobb!) I had been elevated to the sixth grade. But the precious document had been lost in moving from Kansas City to Wayne, Nebraska, and I had only my word of honor and my deceiving appearance (neither at a premium!) to offer as credentials when I appeared before the authorities in the big rambling frame schoolhouse on the hill.

Evidently I presented a novel problem. I was a bashful, towheaded youngster, very small for my advanced age of twelve; and there was no way to communicate the vital information that I had been taught by a goddess and that, in addition, I was much bigger than I looked!

After some tentative shuntings from here to there and some indefinite waiting yonder, I found myself sitting in the office of the principal, Mr. Ashley, a fearsome name to me. He was not in at the moment, but a big boy who was dressed like a man, wore a stiff collar and a tie, and carried an air, was waiting before me. I judged that he had just descended temporarily from the rarefied atmosphere of high school, for the gulf between us was too wide for communication.

Finally the great man bustled into the office and filled it with his presence. He was really a handsome man, and, as I recall him from the height of now, he probably knew it well. There was a breezy sense of self-appreciation about him that gave gusto to his simplest utterances and made them sound important. That is the way I remember him, and there are few men whom I remember more vividly.

He looked the two of us over from aloft, and said, regarding me from beneath heavy brows that beetled, I suppose, "I will take you first. I gather you are the very little boy who thinks he belongs in the sixth grade. Will you tell me why you think so?"

I did tell him, bearing heavily upon the authority of Miss Lobb and her general excellence. At the height of my testimony, when I must have been most eloquent, he turned his head toward the big boy — *and winked!*

That did it. My face burned and I felt sick. When I tried to answer questions put to me, my tongue refused to work.

At length I was given a note which I was to present next morning to the teacher of the third grade!

I did present my note, because my Mother thought someone would find out about me if I went back to school and did my best. But I could not forget that wink, and there I sat overwhelmed by a hopeless sense of injustice. When my turn to read came, I sat staring at my desk, tongue-tied and sick with shame. It was such baby stuff, and no one knew about my little red book on electricity by a great man named Poyser!

After I had sat there for ages doing nothing, the bell rang for recess; and when my line began moving with the general exodus, I moved with it, eager to escape into the friendly open air. But having passed outdoors with the milling mass of youngsters, the dreadful loneliness of the multitude came upon me; and I stood close to the big front steps, wondering if I should make a run for it and go home. But I had been doing a bit of living since my wild retreat from Bryant School, and when I thought about the way my Mother would feel when I came back home, the thought of running scared me more than the thought of sticking it out. Evidently I had begun to learn about the two opposing fears and the obligation to obey the greater one, the fear of being secretly ashamed of one's self. I can think of several times in my life when surrendering to the greater fear did me a very great service.

It was at this point in my history that my luck changed for the better. Just when I was feeling most lonely, most hopelessly isolated from the mass of my fellow youngsters, a boy whom I had never seen before came up and grinned at me with a friendly, toothful grin. He was a little taller than I, huskily built, and about my age. As I came to think of it later, the grin was no mere casual expression, but rather, a built-in feature of his facial pattern. How I came to love it! He had thick dark eyebrows that did not take the trouble to separate above the nose, but ran straight across, giving him a belligerent look that belied the grin.

"I'll play you a game," he said. "Winners keepers, losers weepers."

I had no marbles on me; and when I confessed the lack, he said, "Oh, I'll lend you some, and when you win you can pay me back."

So we made a ring and played. I was fairly handy with a taw, but no expert, and I wondered at the easy shots he missed. I won (or should I say he lost?) and when the bell rang I paid my debt, and we agreed to meet there by the steps after school.

Yes, that was none other than John Elias Weston Chaffee, a prince of pals! (Sixty-five years later, after a long separation, I saw him for the last time—helpless in a wheel chair, but with the same toothful friendly grin upon his face.)

When the brawling tide of youngsters surged back into the school building, I drifted with it, and took my place of shame in the third grade. Only now the shame was gone and there was no fear. I was no longer alone in an absurdly unjust world that didn't care about me. I had a friend, and I would see him again right after the next bell! Let them come on with their baby stuff and silly questions! For the first time in our many adventures together, that reassuring grin of John's had done the trick.

Shortly after we were seated, a sweet-faced young teacher, who said she was Miss Field, asked me to come with her. We went into a little room together and talked about Kansas City and Miss Lobb, and about my little red book by Poyser, and about the steam engine I wanted to make. I did not say anything about the dream, for it seemed only a nightmare yet, and I was sad when I thought of it. She had me read some things for her, and they were easy. Then I said the multiplication tables for her.

After a while she said she would like to have me in her sixth grade!

Miss Field did not quite win a place in the Pantheon of Goddesses along with Miss Lobb; but she almost made it!

28

I remember very little about my life at school that winter when I turned thirteen. I must have had no difficulty with my classwork, for I do not remember studying or reciting, except in a vague way; and at the beginning of the midwinter term I was promoted to the seventh grade.

What I recall most vividly is the writing of my first "poem," entitled "The Stubble-Haired Boy." Certainly it was a juvenile masterpiece—*in reverse!* But it had the undeniable merit of being about something I knew something about—my own uncombed hair and the alleged distress it caused my doting Mother.

I don't know yet why I wanted to do the thing. No one that I knew was poetizing, and I was living in a society wholly absorbed in the honorable business of raising grain, cattle, and hogs to feed the human race. There was no demand for poetry.

I had spent the past summer out on the farm with Uncle George, and had felt the deep tides of that natural life with its hard-won satisfactions. During the wheat harvest, I had ridden the lead horse in the five-horse team that pulled the Buckeye binder. Machinery being expensive and scarce, we cut grain for the neighbors too, thus greatly prolonging the harvest. Twelve to fifteen hours of staying awake and alert on the back of a sweating horse, under the broiling sun, with the binder back yonder humming its monotonous, hypnotic song, was a grueling experience for a boy; but it was a happy one too. I had rejoiced to feel myself a part of that manly way of living and doing. It was a great adventure, and even the excessive thirst and the ravenous hunger seemed romantic.

At first I was very much pleased with my poem, and so were my Mother and sisters. I went about with a glorified feeling because of it.

Then one day when I was reading it again, as one might re-examine a precious possession by way of becoming more keenly aware of the treasure, suddenly the glorified feeling was darkened. What I was reading seemed silly and made me ashamed.

Why, it was no good!

It just wasn't any good!

I read it over and over eagerly, hoping to bring it back. But it was no use. All the virtue had leaked out of it!

So, when no one was looking, I put it in the kitchen stove.

For days thereafter the world seemed dreadfully empty and lonely—like being homesick.

But before long, I was at work on a new poem entitled "Ambition," and it was going to be really good.

I had been reading hungrily in the random collection of books near the teacher's desk, and I was fascinated by the way common words could be put together and made to sing while they were working.

There was a famous poet by the name of Alfred, Lord Tennyson, and he knew how! It thrilled me to recite the following lines of his:

> The rain had fallen, the poet arose,
> He passed by the town and out of the street.
> A light wind blew from the gates of the dawn,
> And waves of shadow ran over the wheat.
> And he sat him down in a lonely place
> And chanted a melody, loud and sweet,
> That made the wild swan pause in her cloud
> And the lark drop down at his feet.

I could never hope to do anything like that, and so I wouldn't try to imitate it. Anyway, being a lord with an ample bardic beard seemed somehow to make the wonder possible, and of course I could never achieve that majestic image. But maybe if I kept on trying all my life I could do something different that was beautiful too. Or, at least, I might be able to make just one line that would be all poetry; and people who cared would read it and be glad that it was a perfect line.

With a sense of compulsion that left me little leisure for ordinary pleasures, I worked and worked on my poem, trying to make it sing a bit while it was saying. Sometimes I wakened in the night and spent several hours with it in the eerie silence of the sleeping house.

After some weeks of incubation, "Ambition" was ready for Posterity—or the cookstove. No doubt it was better than my former effort, and my Mother and sisters liked it immensely! I liked it too—so well that I dared think of publication!

At that time the *Bloomington* (Illinois) *Eye* was a widely distributed weekly, selling at a nickel a copy. Small boys peddled it on the streets, and so took their first brave steps toward

Success (and perhaps even the Presidency!). Why not offer my poem to the *Eye*? I did so, desperately hoping for a miracle.

The miracle occurred! After the lapse of more than three-score years and ten I am still surprised, although no longer delighted. They not only took my poem; they paid for it—with a six months' subscription to the *Eye*!

The poem actually appeared in print—not on the front page, it is true. But there it was along toward the back pages, with my full name attached as big as life!

For a while it was like being famous, I thought. Also, it was vastly encouraging. If the *Eye* liked that one, let it wait until it saw the next one! Already I was beginning to feel the shape of it!

29

It has often been remarked that small events may have large results, even changing the course of history. "For want of a nail the shoe was lost. For want of a shoe the horse was lost. For want of a horse the king was lost. For want . . ." and so on, to the loss of the kingdom. Similarly, because my sisters had been saving soap wrappers, that second poem of mine never appeared in the *Bloomington Eye*. It did not even come through, and is still waiting somewhere on the other side of things, perhaps, for a young poet who has not yet managed to get born. Happily, the accumulation of wrappers had become sufficient to procure several 16mo paperback copies of classics. One of these was *Idylls of the King*, by the very poet whom I had come to hold in awe!

That little book was to be for me the Great Front Gate to the World of Wonder, Wisdom, and Beauty. Many years later, David Starr Jordan, about to introduce me to a waiting Stanford audience, leaned over from his chair beside me on the rostrum and whispered: "Where shall I say you were educated?" I replied, whispering: "Insofar as I *am* educated, it has been through contact with the Great Ones." "That," he said, forgetting to whisper, "is the only way!" I was thinking of that cheap little book when I answered, for, once the gate was open, there was no end to thrilling explorations. Book led to book, seer to seer, poet to poet, until I wandered far through the years from that little Great Front Gate; and I could write with profound conviction:

> With Eld thy chain of days is one.
> The seas are still Homeric seas!
> The sky shall glow with Pindar's sun,
> The stars of Socrates!

And what is education but the process of expanding the individual consciousness to include as much of race consciousness as possible, with universal sympathy as the ideal achievement?

That cheap 16mo is the most precious item in my collections at the University of Missouri Library. The date written across the first page of the dog-eared copy is 1893. I was still twelve years old, about to turn thirteen.

The glory of my near-fame was fading rapidly. Nothing had come of it all, and nobody seemed to care. Also something like an inner voice without words had begun to disparage my triumph: *This much was nothing at all. I must come away. I must not linger. It was far to where we were going, and I must hurry.* That was the substance of the growing mood of compulsion that I felt.

I had, for the first time, experienced the magic of blank verse, words taught to march in such a manner that their very going was like a river of music! My poet could do that; and he could make a noble tale come forth singing out of an enchanted world where great heroes met in desperate battle and beautiful women mourned.

Soon I was trying my hand at this different kind of poetry that seemed as easy as talking, but was somehow very hard to make so that it would sing while it was saying.

And I too would make a story; not, as might have been supposed, about Arthur and his knights and that "last dim battle in the West where all of high and holy died away." My poet had told all that and it was told forever.

No one had ever heard the story I would make to come forth singing. Mine would be about men who lived in caves long before there were any poets in the world. No one had ever heard of my hero either. I know, because I made him up myself one night when I couldn't sleep for the excitement of creation. Also, I gave him a name that no one ever heard before or since. That name became the title of what was to be my very first book. I was busy designing its format before I had a dozen lines of the content. Here is the title page:

CHALBOA

An Epic of the Stone Age

by
John G. Neihardt

———

Dedicated to
John Elias Weston Chaffee
Prince of Pals

———

30

At this point, my memories become broken and dreamlike for a while. I still recall the headlong drive to complete the work before it should be too late. Why too late, I didn't know. The task became a beloved burden day and night. Often I was far away in a Stone Age world when I should have been doing my schoolwork. Sometimes I wakened in the night to work awhile.

There must have been about a thousand lines in *Chalboa*, and yet I can't repeat a single one of them! I can't even quite recall the story, although I gather from what I do remember that it must have been exciting enough. (Fancy big, brawny half-men fighting with stones and clubs!)

I might well conclude that the whole fantastic business was a dream, and that only fragments broke through into this side of sleep. But that could not be true, for often when John and I were on one of our walking trips I chanted the latest passages of *Chalboa* to John and he was convinced that we were witnessing the birth of a masterpiece. (What a pal he was!) And surely when, within a year of its completion, the precious, hardbound volume with its fancy lettering was given to the flames along with various other manuscripts, it flared as brightly as ordinary paper and ended as indubitable ashes.

I had planned *Chalboa* as the first of three related narratives, the second to be called *Tlingilla*, and the third to be entitled *The Wizard of the Wind*.

Tlingilla seems as vaguely dreamlike now as *Chalboa;* yet I know it was written with the same sense of compulsion that I had felt before. I know that it was completed and bound (less ornately than *Chalboa*) and that the heroine is named in the title. There must have been about five hundred pentameter lines; and yet not one of them has survived the Horatian "tooth of time and tongue of fire."

What would I not give for my blank-verse description of that mysterious Lady of the Caves! She must have been sensational, and (recalling Marlowe's Helen and her thousand ships) I have no doubt that her face could have "launched" a sizable flotilla of war canoes!

I dimly recall that *The Wizard of the Wind* was intended to raise the hero and heroine to a higher level of being; but how this was to be done I do not know. Yet the work was as definitely real as the two other narratives, so far as it went. I still can see the manuscript with the title and author's name boldly and very carefully written on the first page. I do not know how much was in the manuscript; but in the burning time that was to come, I saw it burst into flame and end in ashes like the others.

I am certain, however, that I did not complete the narrative. It just seems to have faded away into the common world of actualities.

31

It must have been about this time, while I was still busy with my Cave Man Trilogy, that I made a great discovery. It happened on a dismal, rainy Sunday. My Mother was going through the family trunk, leisurely sorting odds and ends, while I looked on, being housebound and having nothing better to do. My sisters must have been busy with their own affairs somewhere about the house, for they did not share in my discovery.

A red leather billfold, somewhat faded and worn, appeared from under some long-discarded clothing. I recognized it as my Father's, and I must have cried out when I saw it. He used to carry it in the inside breast pocket of his coat, and I often wondered what he kept in it, but it never occurred to me to ask. Surely it couldn't have been money that made it bulge at times!

Then my Mother did a strange thing. Without looking up she gave me the billfold, pressed both my hands tightly about it, and kissed them. Then she got up quickly and went into her bedroom.

I made the great discovery out in the kitchen that afternoon, while the gusty rain beat upon the windows. Along with many scribbled notes that meant nothing to me, there were numerous clippings from newspapers and magazines in the billfold. Several were about Robert G. Ingersoll. One was about Whittier and his schoolhouse sitting by the road. And there was one about the Battle of Wounded Knee. He must have told me about that affair, which had happened while we were living at 2428 Olive Street in Kansas City. I was nine years old, and I remember the vague half-fear that the Indians might come howling down Olive!

In addition to the clippings and scribbled notes, there was a folded sheet of scratch paper. Inside the fold were penciled four rhyming lines of eight-syllable trochaic verse. These had been written out with great care, evidently, and they were signed in a stiffly correct manner with ornate capitals— "Nicholas Nathan Nihart."

I had not known before that my Father ever wrote verse.

The first line was about us children: "I love Johnny, I love Lulu, I love Gracie just as well." All the remainder was about me and my destined "greatness" as an inventor.

It was clearly a love poem, and for years my possession of it was a precious secret. I could not bear to think of showing it to anyone. I *knew* it was a fine poem. It had to be; for I could feel the deep ache of it in the middle of my breast.

But somehow I knew also that the poem wasn't really in the lines—not *really*. And maybe others wouldn't find it.

32

It could not have been long after this that I began hanging around the tombstone shop of "Professor" R. Durrin, near the old Wayne Opera House on upper Main Street. Maybe it was by accident that I came to know the "professor"; but I don't think so. I am halfway convinced that there are dynamic patterns in our cosmos; that somehow some of us are caught up in such patterns and must fulfill them at any cost. I don't know just what I mean; but I suspect that I mean something worthy of consideration. Surely if this be true, I fell into one of the major patterns of my life when I first entered the shop full of tombstones in various stages of becoming—rough and polished, carved and lettered, doves and lilies, lambs and angels.

He was putting the finishing touches on a petrified angel when I stepped inside to take a look at what he was doing, for he was known to be devilish clever with chisel and mallet. Leaning over his work and tapping with great care, he was unaware of my presence for some time. Finally, rising to his full height, he gazed far down upon me, his keen gray eyes slowly coming into seeing focus, as though he had been a long way off and was just getting back. I can see him yet, standing there, over six erect feet of him; and I can see his Raphael face, as finely chiseled as though he had done it himself. He must have been still in his early fifties, and the sprinkling of gray in his tousled dark hair was only marble dust.

Having brought the small barefooted boy into sharp focus, he smiled with a special sort of mock-serious smile he had and said: "Well, well! It's the fellow who writes poetry, they say!" No doubt at this point I looked guilty and apologetic. "But don't feel too bad about it," he continued. "Some very great men have done it. I even do it myself now and then!"

Suddenly that long-focus look came back into his eyes, and he seemed to have forgotten me as he turned back to his angel and began tapping intently and ever so lightly. For some time he worked in silence, now and then stepping back a pace to appraise the effect of his gentle tapping. This went on so long that I was about to go on my way, for I was on an errand for my Mother at the time and had just looked in curiously on passing.

I had started for the door when he wakened on a sudden to my presence. "By the way," he said, still gazing at the angel, "you wouldn't be wanting a job, I suppose? How about learning to polish marble? I could use a polisher."

Now turning upon me the full candlepower of a kindly

gaze that I later learned to love, he added: "We could talk about poetry while we worked, you know; and maybe spout it to each other. Eh?"

There was nothing at the moment that I wanted so much as to be a marble-polisher; so I was hired on the spot—just like that!

I have tried to remember if I ever actually received wages in coin of the realm, but memory fails me here; and, anyway, that was a trivial matter in the enchanted world of long vistas that I had entered.

The professor was certainly a conspicuous town character, respected, with some condescending reservations, for his unquestioned skill. Yet he was regarded, nonetheless, as a comic figure by those who did not know him, which is to say practically the entire village population. Indeed, they had their reasons. For instance, consider the spectacle when he made his routine excursion to the post office on nice days. Surely, it was something to see the tall, stately man with the tousled hair curling out from under his silk top hat, striding down the street, apparently oblivious of the human race, his piercing gaze fixed on distant vacuity, the tail of his cutaway coat flapping in the breeze he made!

Or maybe there were days when the walking was not so good, and the professor would be seen at mail-time (complete with top hat and cutaway) riding down Main Street in an elderly one-horse buggy, pulled by "old Bill" at a mincing dogtrot. Bill was as much a town character as his doting master. There were floating stories of his mysterious clairvoyant powers, one alleging that Bill needed no guidance in his goings and comings about town, but could read his master's mind and make straight for the desired objective, unerring as a homing pigeon. And there were rumors to the effect that, on various occasions, the professor had been seen earnestly conversing with his horse as man to man.

When I had come to know the professor well and had learned to appreciate his peculiar mock-serious sense of humor, I wondered if perhaps he was only ribbing the natives for his private entertainment—and theirs.

64

Even I — boy that I was — became aware that there were undisclosed chapters in the professor's life story. He spoke freely, and with some pride, of his experience as a student under Thomas Buchanan Read, the once celebrated poet and sculptor. Occasionally, in unguarded moments, there were hints of better days; and his work, scattered helter-skelter through the cluttered tombstone shop, made one wonder what he was doing in our village. There were masterly drawings on marble plaques done by a process of his own invention. There were beautifully wrought bas-reliefs and sculptured figures that drew much dust and little attention.

Only once, so far as I can remember, did he speak of personal matters to me. This was some time after our first meeting. We were both working in silence, I at a polishing job and he carefully tapping out an epitaph. We had been silent for an unusually long time when he straightened up and turned his still-unfocused eyes upon me. Then he began quoting some stanzas from a sentimental poem. I remember the concluding lines:

> O that the players might go on playing
> And we waltz on to the vast Forever,
> Where no hearts break and no ties sever,
> And nobody goes away.

When he had finished, he turned again to his careful tapping and there was a long silence. Then again he turned his blank gaze on me, and asked if I had ever heard of Ella Wheeler. I told him I had; that everybody had heard of Ella Wheeler Wilcox because of her book, *Poems of Passion*. "John," he said, "she nearly became Ella Wheeler Durrin, but her folks didn't like me. They said I was no good. I sometimes wonder if they were right, John. She wrote that poem the night after I left Delovan, our home town, for good."

He was silent for a long while, apparently intent upon carving in imperishable marble a soon-to-be-forgotten tale.

At length he ceased tapping, and, turning on me a mock-tragic countenance, he said, his voice trembling as with suppressed grief: "John, I have composed poor old Bill's epitaph, for surely he will need one before long; and here it is." In the grand manner, with all the swells pulled out, he gave forth like an inspired ham doing Shakespeare a favor.

> Here lies Bill,
> The damned old pill,
> The horse that was so lazy.
> With the point of his nose,
> And the tips of his toes
> Turned up to the roots of a daisy.

Wiping his eyes on the back of his hands, he continued with his graven message to posterity.

It was conceivably true, as he once remarked to me, that he could make anything he could see in imagination. Once it was a life-size figure of a charming little boy, carved out of Carrara marble, simply for the joy of working with the precious stuff he loved—and that stuff was expensive! Once it was a pistol with ornately carved grip and shoulder stock, the barrel being wrought from the tine of a hayrake. It was not only a thing of beauty; it was accurate. Done as a labor of love, this was given to Mrs. Durrin for a Christmas present; and it was good to witness her childish delight with the gift, although it is doubtful that she knew which end was the muzzle!

And now let us meet this third and most important member of the family triumvirate, her ladyship, Mrs. Durrin. I never heard her first name, if indeed she had one, which is hard to imagine. *What!* Call her Annie, or Katy, or Beth, or Jennie? or even Adeline?! It could not be done! Even the adoring professor invariably addressed her as "Mrs. Durrin"; and she quite as religiously called him "Professor." I do not attempt to spell the word phonetically in keeping with the lady's rich Virginia accent. Inherited from who knows how many ghostly ancestors, it was mellowly musical; and when she spoke to her great man, there was adoration in her voice and eyes.

As for the professor's response to her idolatry, it was heart-warming to see the benevolent way he looked down upon her, his face glowing with amused affection and pride.

There were some who joked about her pronounced devotion to her man, and those might add a jocular remark or two about her royal forays into the plebeian world — rather overdressed, perhaps (or should one say "arrayed"?).

Neighbor women were never able to achieve a coffee-borrowing, fresh-bread-sharing familiarity with the lonely lady. There were discussions about the probable origin of her obviously expensive turnouts, the consensus favoring the rich-relative-back-home hypothesis.

I can see her yonder far away, a bit dimmed by the mist of time — or is it the Vergilian "tears of things"? I can see her in gorgeous raiment holding earnest conference with the embarrassed butcher over a dime's worth of three-cent boiling meat, like as not, and maybe a free slice or two of liver ("if it's nice and fresh"). I can see her in an evening gown out driving in her carriage (the elderly buggy) on a pleasant afternoon. I see her sitting stiffly like a statue. I see old Bill, half asleep in the shafts, performing faithfully with an air of patient boredom.

And I see that adoration in her eyes.

I see that look again, and I am no longer amused; but I wonder. Was it all not clowning vanity, as we supposed, but rather a desperate striving to seem worthy of the greatness she adored?

33

And that was the family triumvirate: the professor, old Bill, and the adoring Mrs. Durrin.

But there was another tripartite power in our little gravestone world. Or should we call it "the Trinity," as the professor insisted in one of his mock-serious, irreverent moods? "Anyone can see," he said, "that the judge there is the Father. I am quite as clearly the Son-of-a-Gun. And you, John, with your spooky poetizing, can be none other than the Holy Ghost!"

But who was the judge? you are thinking.

Well, when I first saw Judge James Brittain among the gravestones, discoursing about some great Shakespearean actor he had known, I was disappointed — not in the man, but in the lack of a toga. For he looked the way a Roman senator looked in the days when Roman senators looked the way they should have looked.

He was comfortably over the high divide of middle age, but not yet gaining momentum on the downhill slide. He had dignity, poise, and a quiet air of distinction. Anyone seeing him would know that he was, or had been, or could be, somebody in particular. And when he spoke it was as one having authority. As I look back upon those days in the light of all I have learned to value since then, I feel that he must have been a richly literate man. He was especially fond of the drama. The Elizabethans were his buddies, and he could recite Shakespeare by the hour. Sometimes he did, when we were busy with the quieter stages of marble-polishing; and it was a thrilling experience to hear his well-modulated, dark-brown voice making the pentameters come gloriously alive!

"Judge Brittain's home" was one of the larger houses of our town, and no doubt it was imposing before it had needed paint so long. The judge was still owner and proprietor of our "opera house" on upper Main Street, previously mentioned in this history. It was his Temple of the Drama, reverently, if overgenerously, built with the dregs of a once considerable fortune. Traveling shows still held forth there, now and then. There were political rallies in season, and occasional dances; but the Temple was usually "dark"; and it too was needing paint.

Now and then the judge would speak hopefully of his property in Duluth. "When Duluth property comes back," he would begin; and then he would tell of some benevolent or cultural scheme he had in mind and heart. While I was working on my *The Divine Enchantment,* it was that little book he would "put over—when Duluth—"

Well, Duluth property *did* finally "come back"—when one of our imperishable marbles bore his name.

It should be easy to believe that our Tombstone Trinity attracted some attention in our sensible community—the dignified judge, lacking only the senatorial toga; the stately, eagle-eyed professor with his occasional top hat and cutaway; and the undersized, white-headed boy in his early teens, "who writes poetry, they say." We must have provoked some derisive gaiety when we were seen together on the street; and curious, drop-in visitors at the shop could have reported sketchily heard discourse and argument on matters totally unrelated to common sense. I heard that there were those who deplored the degrading influence of "those godless old codgers" on "that little boy." Even my Grandmother, whose sturdy pioneer virtues have been celebrated in this history, took me severely to task. "Oh, John, if you would only quit reading them Hoodoo books, them awful Hoodoo books!" And I was shamelessly guilty, being deeply interested in Hindu religion and Vedanta philosophy. The judge had found books for me in his private library—including a little volume of Upanishads, which he gave me and I still cherish. The professor had loaned me *The Bible in India* by Jacolliot, a French judge and scholar. It was the latter book that gave me the scheme of my *The Divine Enchantment.*

Truly, there must have been some good talk there among the gravestones; but there were nasty rumors abroad to the effect that we were "downright infidels"; and that was a fearsome thing to be in those pious days when all the answers were still well known to the faithful!

34

Honest, I feel ashamed of the next episode.

Then why write it?

Because I must live up to the noble role of historian that I have assumed. I must "hew to the line and let the best man fall where he may," if I remember the saying correctly.

I was deep in the cosmic dream of the Virgin Devanaguy when the impudently mundane event came to pass. It should be noted here that the virgin was carrying her unborn son, Krishna, who was being prepared for his future earthly duties as savior by the divinely inspired dreams of his mother. (This will give some idea of the depths of degradation to which "that little boy" had fallen.)

I had recently finished the "Interlude," which consisted of four Spenserian stanzas and served as a link between the two sections of the *Enchantment.* I had always been almost superstitiously afraid to read my work to anyone while it was in progress; but good Spenserian stanzas were hard to come by, and I was especially elated over mine. So I read them to the professor and the judge.

When I had finished, neither spoke a word for what seemed a cruelly long while, and I feared that I had failed. Finally the judge came over to me with bowed head and hands extended and the professor, turning his benevolently glowing smile upon me, said: "John, I don't see how you do it!" Although I was all of fifteen years old at the time, that was the greatest praise I had received in all my life.

So "the evening and the morning were the Seventh Day," and having looked upon my work, I saw that it was good!

But it was at precisely this exalted moment of my history that I fell from grace, and this is how it was.

Our community was in the throes of a spiritual revival again, and our population was being sharply divided into two categories, namely, the Righteous, with their monopoly of virtue, and the Unrighteous, with a comfortable majority and most of the fun.

The process of segregation was mounting feverishly toward a climactic fury, and the heavenly Indian-summer evenings had been greatly troubled by the strident oratory of an angry prophet proclaiming woe for the faithless. The prophetic voice belonged to one Reverend Cordner and it emanated from a spacious tent pitched on the vacant lots back of the tombstone shop.

John and I had decided to attend the services; not with contrite hearts, certainly; for, as a matter of fact, Hell had no terrors for us. We were still thoroughly enjoying our various iniquities; and we had no serious changes in mind. It was, rather, a Tom Sawyerish spirit of adventure that moved us; and we had heard weird tales.

Upon entering the tent, the mind of the candidate for redemption was immediately shocked into a receptive state by a realistic, even horrendous, picture of flaming Hell. It was painted in lurid, living colors on a ten-foot canvas suspended at the speaker's end of the tabernacle; and, according to reports, it had served admirably to illustrate and reinforce the reverend's diatribes on Sin and his graphic forecasts of Eternal Damnation.

It had been a weather-breeding day, and that evening there was an ominous feel in the sky-wide stillness, as of a breathless waiting for something to begin.

The shrill voice of the prophet took wings and fled far out into the empty hush.

The air had cooled but little with the sunset, and the unseasonal heat seemed the more oppressive in recalling the sharp frost of a week before.

As we entered, the stuffy swelter of the crowded tent seemed to radiate from the pictured bonfire of the damned up yonder. During the recent brief cold snap, straw had been littered under the chairs for the comfort of the congregation's feet. It made the place feel hotter; and there was no relief in the fact that the side curtains of the tent had been removed.

There was a great outpouring of the spirit that evening. Surely there were young men seeing visions in that tent and old men dreaming dreams! Stubborn sinners all their lives

71

broke down, confessing, and "came forward," unashamed to weep for their sins. Praise the Lord! Hallelujah!

And there was tremendous lifting power in the hymns—as of mighty wings outspread—when the whole congregation gave forth as with one full-throated voice.

Led by the calisthenics and the strained tenor of the sweating prophet, they were singing, with a glorious surge of power, "Swing open, fair portal, one moment and let us look through. One moment we falter immortal—"

And truly it was as though we faltered deathless, in a moment of ecstatic song, before the Gate of Heaven.

John and I had forgotten to giggle and nudge each other, moved vaguely, perhaps, by the sad soul's world-old longing to go home.

And then it happened!

Suddenly the cold front struck out of the Northwest with a swirling gust that made the stricken canvas boom and bellow, the tent poles sway and groan.

The wingéd song died abruptly in a tumult of panic voices, blended by terror into a high-pitched screaming.

The prophet, true to his faith, still kept his pulpit, shouting to his frenzied congregation; but few, save those about the altar, paused to listen: *Did they not trust the Lord? Was this the measure of their faith? Had he not preached for years in the windy state of Kansas? And never had the Lord allowed his tent to be damaged! Let them have faith and keep their seats! Have faith and praise the Lord!*

But the stakes were giving way to windward and the tent roof bulged and slatted furiously. Driven with the dust and straw, we, all of us—the righteous and the damned—were of a single addled mind, to "get the hell outside of there," as someone eloquently phrased it, "before the [censored] tent came down!"

Well, we, all of us, did get outside, thanks to the removal of the side curtains; and the tent did collapse.

Even the stubborn reverend made it safely. Leaving last, like a good skipper, he was seen crawling out of the wreckage just before the shattered coal-oil lamps found the straw, and a realistic little hell broke loose for sure!

35

The fiery spectacle drew well and was, on the whole, a popular success.

All next day the curious drifted in from miles around to view the wreckage of charred chairs, provide illuminating comment, and dispense belated wisdom. Some of the more civic-minded called for a law forbidding the use of tents for public meetings. Others, with shrewd, knowing looks, agreed that "some of us around here ain't been livin' right." A few of the newly redeemed, unawed by tribulation, would start a fund at once to restore the ruined tabernacle.

But somehow the tale had got started (and it was growing still) about the prophet's frantic scolding of his flock for want of faith and his boast of special favor with the Lord. The wicked made the most of the story! Profane slogans grew up among the godless—like *Hallelujah! What's your hurry? Hell's apoppin', praise the Lord!* A couple of barbershop cutups brought forth a mock-pious hymn sung soulfully with blended minors.

Meanwhile there was some hilarity among the gravestones. Since no one was hurt in the holocaust, there seemed to be no cause for sorrow. And the story of the reverend's predicament did seem to have some comic aspects, at the time!

As for my shameful part in the unfortunate affair, it was "those old codgers," the professor and the judge, who put me up to it; and, after all, I was only an innocent little boy of about fifteen!

"John, here is the opportunity of a lifetime!" said the judge, or words to that effect. "Why not immortalize the Reverend Cordner in his war against the Legions of Sin? Think of his single combat with Satan on the embattled plains of Nebraska! And that final terrific scene when the holy citadel goes up in flames!"

"Yes, yes!" the professor agreed with enthusiasm. "It will be a great epic poem like Homer and Milton used to write! We will call it 'The Tentiad,' and Goldie will leap at the chance to print it!"

And who was Goldie?

W. S. Goldie was the intellectual bad boy of our town. His weekly paper, the *Nebraska Democrat,* was generally regarded as somewhat of a "scandal sheet," but everybody read it— especially the righteous, it was said, and they declared it ought to be excluded from the mail!

Goldie was an iconoclast in the great age of iconoclasm, when Brann of Waco, Texas, was still the recognized high priest of that crusade against the smug, the respectable, the established. He was a picturesque figure, often pointed out to strangers on the street. Tall, erect, handsome, with black locks curling around his ears, he did look the genius that he was supposed to be, and probably was—a genius who had "missed the boat" somewhere along the way.

It was a Saturday morning with a clear weekend ahead. So, encouraged by such backing and still a bit exalted by my recent triumph with the "Interlude," I began forthwith to build my epic, surrendering completely to the divine afflatus. The small back room of the shop was dedicated to my use. They brought me sandwiches at noon, and a glass of water at reasonable intervals. All day long I toiled. At home I continued far into the night. All next day I did not cease until nightfall.

Then I had it—all neatly written out for posterity!

That was over seventy years ago, and I cannot repeat a single line of that opus. I do remember more or less vague portions of the idiotic plot—for instance, the Prophet's single combat with the Devil, witnessed by the serried hosts of Good and Evil! More vividly I recall the grand finale, when the Prophet's hell-fire speech against the Wicked ignites the very straw! Whereat Jehovah, only wishing to be helpful to his Servant, summons all Four Winds to blow the conflagration out—and greatly worsens matters!

Here I can point with pride to the pious ending, when the all but martyred Servant of the Lord is rescued by divine intervention from his own too realistic hell!

Mind you, I am not saying that all of this was really very funny. I am only saying it was fun.

Goldie published *The Tentiad* with a grand flourish—impudently conspicuous on the front page, two brazen columns of it!

So I woke one morning and found myself infamous. According to reports there was unholy glee among the unregenerate; but the righteous disapproved vociferously, viewing my work with alarm. A local minister declared the author ought to be escorted out of town!

I have hunted high and low for that issue, but it is missing in the only files I know.

36

During the late 1880's, something like a cultural epidemic spread across the Middle West. The country was emerging from its pioneer period, and it was beginning to hunger for what William James called the "more."

Communities scattered here and there across the land were more or less violently attacked. A raggedy small town, for instance, might be seized with an irrational desire to have a higher institution of learning for its very own. Previously, it had been concerned chiefly with the drab business of making a living, in spite of drouths, grasshoppers, hailstorms, high interest rates, and starvation prices for corn and hogs. But now it had seen, and would follow, the Gleam.

Whereupon, another "academy" erupted into being from

the dust of the earth! Some of these survived by virtue of faith, hope, and the limited charity of moneylenders. A few even grew into distinguished institutions. Others went the way of dreams.

But the Subtle Influence outlived its epidemic stage. And that, by the grace of God, is where I came in!

I first became acquainted with the "academy" story shortly after John Chaffee and I had found each other, as already related in this history. We two were on one of our exploratory walking trips. Returning home across the fields as a crow flies, ignoring roads and fences as impertinent interruptions, we were approaching the Wayne cemetery from the northern side when we came upon a flourishing patch of weeds. They were taller than average weeds, and they were huddled close together as though guarding some precious secret.

Here was a mystery to be solved! Thrilled with the spirit of adventure, we pushed through the tight cordon of weeds and stood staring — at a big hole in the ground. Clearly it had once been squared, and therefore it was fashioned by men; but the walls were slanted by frost and rain and wind. Several dressed stones were lying round about in desultory fashion.

Being in a romantic mood and not far from a burial ground, we agreed that the hole looked like a giant's grave without the giant. And truly something great had been buried there awhile for, as we later learned, we had found the basement of the "Wayne Academy" that never got out of the ground!

37

But the grave was open indeed! The resurrected Spirit of the Academies was abroad again, and it had been working wonders in our town.

Two practical visionaries had come to Wayne out of the

East with an evangelical purpose — to found a teachers college that would help to spread the light of learning along the developing frontier. They were James Madison Pile and Ulysses S. Conn. It is with love and reverence that I write their names, for they were great-hearted, great-spirited men, and my debt to them is a precious thing to me.

With boundless faith and the proverbial shoestring, backed by local loyalties and some grudging credit in a time of tight money, they had undertaken to build the Nebraska Normal College.

And lo! yonder now it soared from a barren, treeless hilltop at the northeast edge of town. An impossible dream had come true. Who said it couldn't be done? There it was! And what a magnificent example of architecture!

It was built of red brick, three stories high, counting the full basement that was less than half below ground level. Several rooms in the attic were used as a men's dormitory. A square bell tower on the southwest corner dominated the whole. Truly it was something to show with pride to visiting strangers!

And then the generously planned interior! The library, the classrooms, and the office on the first floor. On the second, the chapel, the gymnasium, and the bell-tower room, which was to be my very own for several glorious years.

And the grand stairway leading from the front entrance past the great windows, two stories high. Surely that was something to see!

Pending the opening of the new building, the early sessions of the institution had been held in a small, false-front frame shack on Main Street, about a block and a half south of the tombstone shop. The faculty consisted of Professors Pile and Conn. Student enrollment could hardly have exceeded a dozen — in any case, too many for simultaneous attendance.

My Uncle Charles Culler, who became a notable educator, was a member of the first class — a hard-won triumph for him. As a little boy in Kansas, I had seen him sitting under an umbrella on the sun-baked buffalo grass, watching the

77

family livestock at graze and poring over some borrowed text-book. Someday, somehow, he would go to college. Someday, somehow, he was going to be a teacher.

And there he was, a college man at last! It wasn't Princeton, but it *was* college.

38

A life story is not to be likened to a simple river of events and moods. Rather it is a complex of various streams, flowing roughly in parallel, and apparently related only by their common direction.

Thus, all the while I have been remembering, there were collateral happenings that must be recalled; and I find it impossible to fit all parts of the story into one neat, chronological pattern. Sometimes a vivid picture jostles an equally vivid picture, as though vying for position at a single point of time. How could I have been there when I was here or yonder? How could I have been doing this and that at one time? Yet surely all of it was lived. I can tell as I remember, and the principal dates are clear.

The troubled story of my continuing education, as the reader will recall, was left dangling somewhere in the upper reaches of the Wayne Grade School. There a fog shuts down for me, for at this point Miss Field vanished from my world. Whether it was death or marriage or just going away I do not know; but it was fatal for my learning in that school. The place had been jinxed from the beginning, and now it was hopeless.

If I ever studied or recited after that, I have no memory of it. The point to being there at all was to endure—until recess, until noon, until recess, and then, at last, until the school let out at four. Best of all was the glad last day, with a whole free summer ahead! And maybe something would happen and school would never begin again!

For some time I had been working, more or less, on my Cave Man Trilogy—on weekends, sometimes, when I was not at the tombstone shop; often at nights, and during school hours when I should have been studying.

When school closed that spring, John and I hired out to work in sugar-beet fields at seventy-five cents for a ten-hour day. At first the job seemed easy enough. You had only to straddle a row stretching God knows how far ahead, and crawl, thinning blocks of little sugar-beet plants and pulling weeds as you went along. It was not an unpleasant job before your wrists began to creak rustily and your fingertips became like incipient boils. And then how the sun did beat down on your back!

It helped to realize how very much all this might mean. Figure it out and see. Four dollars and fifty cents for every week of six ten-hour days. Think how many weeks in a summer. And how the money would pile up if you didn't spend a nickel until fall. It would pay much rent and buy a lot of coal and groceries.

Thinking about the Cave Man Trilogy was a great help too. I could work on it while I was pulling weeds and beets. The poem was being written in blank verse, and there were many minor technical problems to solve. I could think of these quite as well on all fours as when sitting up; and when I lost myself in the poem for a while, my wrists and fingertips no longer troubled me, and the whole adventure became glorious.

The fabulous sum, however, is still at the rainbow's end beyond an interminable row of beets and beets and beets.

39

When the cultivators laid the crop by, there was no longer any need for crawling boys. So John and I hoed wild morning-glory patches in a cornfield at fifty cents a day. The bottom had dropped out of the young labor market, and boys were selling at a dime a dozen. After *swinking* in the corn for several days, we decided there was no percentage in the morning-glory business and we ought to go hunting for a real job. Maybe if we separated and went alone — and far — each of us might find a farmer who had been looking for just the sort of hired hands that we could be.

So one morning we set out from town in opposite directions, carrying sandwiches that our mothers had put up for us. They would come in handy at noon before we began talking to farmers.

We had agreed to continue walking at about the rate of four miles per hour until the sun was straight up. Then, after eating and resting, we would begin working on the farmers along the way. Maybe in an entirely strange community we would be judged as the almost-men we really were, and not as the little boys we used to be.

John and I were good walkers, and proud of the fact. We could clip off our four miles per hour by the watch, and keep it up for hours. We often did it just to prove again that we could.

So I turned loose at top speed, swinging along hopefully, the country getting stranger and stranger. As I penetrated deeper and deeper into the region of opportunity, I made up conversations that the farmers and I would soon be having. Of course, the first one would not need a hand, because he had just hired one that very morning. But the next one! — well, how much would I have to get for my work? That was a poser, and what would I say? If I said too much, he would not take me. If I said too little, then I'd be sorry. But maybe the farmer would need me so much that he would make me a surprising offer, and I would take it at once. Then I could hurry back home and tell John and my Mother.

Finally, when I had rested, sitting at the roadside, and eaten my sandwiches, I said to myself, "There is a house just beyond that hill yonder, and that is where I will begin."

There *was* a house on the other side, just as I had thought! This seemed a good omen. But when I looked at the house, I was scared. It was clearly a rich man's home. The ample barns and sheds—all gleaming with white paint—also indicated a wealthy owner.

My heart was up in my throat, but I had promised myself I would begin there, so I had to do it; and I did.

Some neighbor had driven up in a wagon, and no doubt a discussion of the weather was in progress. The two eyed me curiously as I stood there, wondering how to begin. Finally the man on the ground, who must have been the rich owner, said, "Well, young man, and where are *you* going?"

I explained. You see, I was just passing by and I thought I would drop in and see if he could use a hired hand.

The two men looked at each other and grinned.

No-o-o-o. He really didn't need a man just then. He was sorry, but maybe another time if I happened to be passing.

Well, I was just passing by, and I thought I'd stop and ask. Good-by.

As I passed through the front gate at a brisk dogtrot, I heard them laugh back yonder. The sound further reduced my courage, but I let on I didn't care. That was the way it was, hunting a job, and you had to keep on trying.

When I came to the next house, my heart failed me completely. I stood gazing at the rich, happy home, trying to make myself go in, but it was no use. By now I was seeing myself the way those men back there had seen me. It would be the same here.

So I started off down the road, feeling an utter outsider rejected by a world of fortunate strangers. Home was the only place to go, but I could not pass the first rich house again. I must go around a whole section to avoid being seen yonder. That made it two miles farther, but I was in no hurry now with what I had to tell.

As the distance increased between me and the scene of my shame, I managed to regain much of my self-respect by thinking about my book. What *would* those men say if they could

81

only know! It was especially comforting to imagine how we might meet again in some far-off future. They would be old, old men; and almost everybody would know about my books by that time. Maybe we would have a good laugh together. It might be something like this:

—*Do you remember when I came to your house and offered to be your hired man?*

—*And you were such a little kid! Ha! Ha! Ha! Ha!*

—*And you were sorry, but you couldn't use another man just then! Ha! Ha! Ha!*

—*Those were the days, weren't they!*

And maybe after that we would be good friends all the rest of our lives.

John was already at home when I arrived. His story was no better than mine.

40

It looked like the end of the trail for me; but it was only another and better beginning.

My Mother had been sewing for Mrs. Pile and her daughter at their home in the basement of the college on the hill. One day at dinner the professor had asked her what she was planning to do with that boy of hers. That was exactly the question she had been asking herself; and, as yet, there had been no answer.

After some discussion of the subject, the professor said, "Why don't you send him up here to us? We need a bell ringer, and he could ring the bell for his tuition. If you like the idea, send him along and I'll have a talk with him."

So with some misgivings, I went to see the great Professor James Madison Pile.

I had been waiting in his office for some time when he blew in like a gust of fresh air. The place seemed to come vibrantly alive; and far from being overawed by his presence, I felt safe and liked him at once. Shaking hands with me as though I were a man, he said, "You are Mrs. Neihardt's son John, and you want to talk about ringing our bell."

That being granted, he plunged into the business at hand, plying me with questions about my schooling, my reading, what I thought about this and that, and what I meant to be when I grew up. I told him everything except about the book I was writing, and I'm sure my Mother had told him something about that.

Finally he said he thought I would make a good bell ringer, if I really wanted the job. I would have to ring the bell twice every fifty minutes, beginning at six-thirty in the morning and ending at six in the evening, except on Saturdays and Sundays. This would not be easy, especially in the dark, cold winter mornings; and the whole college would be depending on me for the beginning and ending of classes. All the while I would be going to school myself, and I could learn as fast as I was able and wanted to learn.

He took both my hands in his and looked into my eyes for a while. Then he spoke in a low voice, as though what he said was just for the two of us.

Do you really want to learn, Johnny?

Oh yes, sir; I do, sir. And I wouldn't mind if the job got hard, because my chum and I were always doing things almost too hard to do—like walking twenty miles without food or water, just to see if we could do it!

Then I should be at the college on the first Monday in September, ready to begin; and we would all work and learn together.

41

When I left the college that day, I actually felt much taller and stronger. I was no longer really just a boy pretending to be a man. I was definitely somebody in my own right, for I had a real job with something very important to do.

Think of it! All of those people would need me, and I must never fail them. They would be listening all day, and my bell would tell them when to get up, when to eat, and what to do next. I would have to be very careful not to make a mistake or forget when to ring.

It was still July, and the threshers would be coming to my Uncle's farm to thresh his wheat out of the shock. It would be better than a circus to be out there with them and share the lighthearted carnival spirit that I had experienced the year before. Also I wanted to tell my Uncle and Grandparents my great news. John had gone with his father, a carpenter and contractor, and I was alone for the rest of the summer. There would be work that I could do out there—like helping with the chores and carrying drinking water to the field. I would be paying my way while having a good time.

So I set out afoot for the farm, a hilly, seven-mile jaunt over rutted roads. John and I had made it in two hours, but the way I was feeling, I'd be setting a record this time. We had read that a thousand paces made a mile for the Roman legions; and it was one of our ambitions to equal the stride of Caesar's soldiers. Heel and toe, heel and toe, with a brisk spring from toe to heel—that was the way to do it! And surely I must be doing it. Why, half the time both my feet were off the ground together!

How I surged along, and with what a masterly swing!

Did I not have an important job? And was I not going to college in September?

No more common school! No more common school!

Heel and toe, heel and toe—with a spring from toe to heel!

And a thousand to a mile, a thousand to a mile! Heel and toe!

84

42

Remembering the summers out on Uncle George's farm, I wonder what has happened to the human race since then! Can it be that we were wiser, knowing less? Or happier, with a little valued more? Or is it merely later than I think, and am I getting older than I know?

Anyway, it is like a brief sojourn in Eden to recall the way it was out there that enchanted summer of '94.

There is my Grandfather with his quiet, sobersided wit and the twinkle in his bright blue eyes; a bit slow-footed, maybe, and walking with a stoop reminiscent of uncounted horses shod, but still the old magician at his forge.

There is my Grandmother, still patiently busy and always helping, still radiating the old sense of soft-bosomed, comforting goodness.

There is my ageless Uncle George with his merry banter, a hero for his way with horses, and his knowing, easy way of doing whatever needed doing. And was he not once champion cornhusker of our county? Why, they say that when a husked ear struck the bangboard, he always had another in the air and already on the way! I was proud that I could sometimes beat him in our sweet-corn-eating contests, when each strove manfully to produce the longer row of stripped-off corncobs to prove his prowess. How it delighted him to see a hungry boy eat!

And there is my worshiped Aunt, my Uncle George's wife, newly a mother and sweet with nursing, a born ally of boys, and pretty as Miss Field—almost! And there is the baby, Tommy, whom I often rocked to sleep. He and I became such buddies that he regarded my singing voice as perfectly magnificent—even though I deliberately committed vocal mayhem in a rusty-hinge soprano, out of tune. I am sure of this, because his loudest indictments of the cockeyed world ceased abruptly when I broke out in full song. Except for the way he smiled and gurgled with appreciation, it might have been amazement that he felt. I lived to know him as an old man, retired after a career as locomotive engineer on crack trains bound for the Coast and back — a boyhood dream come true.

Yes, I know the "Drouth of '94" was a weather classic such as old men recall to make a story. And I myself saw the corn blades curl in the searing gale, turn yellow, wither, blow away. Indeed, that wasn't Eden; it was more like Kansas.

But it's quite another picture that I see first when I remember and last when I forget. Merciful evening has come at long last. The booming wind has gone down with the heat-pale sun. A horizon-wide hush has fallen with the darkness. The stars look "old and full of sleep."

No use trying to sleep indoors. The house is like an old Dutch oven ready for the dough. Although the prairie seems to pant with heat left over from the day, it's easier breathing in the open air.

So we are all together there in the starlight, lounging on blankets spread out on the grass: Grandpa and Grandma, Aunt and Uncle with Tommy in his cradle; old Shep, all tongue and panting, stretched out in un-doglike abandonment to misery and unmindful of the cats that have come to share our unfamiliar doings and be people for a while. It's hot, breathless hot! But there's a lifting sense of holiday release about it all, of equality in sharing calamitous experience, a feel of perilous freedom from the humdrum tyrannies of common things.

Along the vague horizon north and west, heat lightning flares by fits — flash on flash of star-devouring brilliance. It should be a rainstorm working up. The big ones come from there; but there's no wisp of cloud. We watch the ghostly storms of light and listen hard for thunder far away.

There! There!

But only tremendous silence trails the flashes.

The ghostly storms grow more remote and dimmer, glimmer awhile beneath the prairie rim, and cease.

— Then, suddenly the cool white of early morning and the vacant sky.

That's what I remember first and last from the Drouth of
'94 — all of us together there, immortal in the starlight.

43

The break of the year came in mid-August with a change of
the wind to the Northwest, a great show of rolling black
clouds, and a sudden drop in temperature. Often such a
break ushered in a long, sodden downpour; but no rain fell.

It was a good time for taking care of the wheat; and for
several days there had been big doings on our farm. We had
been getting ready for the threshers; and threshing, before
the world grew old and wise, was in our country more than a
means of separating grain from straw. That function was
merely important, and so was taken for granted. But the
term "threshing" had developed rich overtones and had come
to signify something like a movable feast, dedicated to the
principle that hard work could be a lot of fun when a number
of friendly people did it together.

This sounds like an ideology — but the only word we had
for it was neighborliness.

First of all, the sitting room had to be transformed into a
dining room, with an improvised table sufficiently large for the
threshing diners. Let's see — how many would there be? Count
them: For the first table — four haulers, two for the power
teams, one each for the band cutter, the feeder, the machinist,
the straw stacker; and surely there would be several more
who would just drop in to help in a general way — and be
invited to "set up and have a bite."

Then there would be the womenfolk who would come over
to help with the cooking and other preparations. But these
would be busy serving and waiting on tables until the men
were through and went out to lounge in the shade for a while
before resuming work. The parlor organ would have to be
moved into the bedroom to make more space for the guests

and the waitresses, who were also hostesses. Windows and screen doors were covered with crisp new mosquito bar to cope with the fly problem. This served also as decoration, giving the place a starchy, dressed-up, holiday look.

It was my special privilege to loiter around the summer kitchen where experts in cookery practiced their arts over a hot cookstove. If any errand was to be run, I ran it—proud to be a part of so worthy a project. If water was to be fetched, I fetched it from the bucket well in the front yard. If the women wanted something canned from the cave, I brought it up out of the cool bowels of the earth. (Which reminds me of the lonely but comfortable hours I spent in the chilly twilight of that cave, churning butter that seemed stubbornly determined not to "come.") Of course all of these activities of mine ceased abruptly upon the arrival of the threshing outfit.

My Uncle had cut his wheat with a Buckeye binder, jointly owned by a group of neighbors including himself, and shocked it in the field for threshing in the late summer or fall. Some farmers stacked their bundled wheat and threshed it the next spring, thus selling, generally, when the market was up, clearing the stubble fields for fall plowing, and also allowing the grain to "go through the sweat," a process which was said to result in a quality superior for the making of flour.

I never learned whether this was folklore or fact; but I do know that stacking bundled grain was something of a fine art in the great good days of old-fashioned threshing. That was before the combine came in and substituted a single man with an oilcan and a monkey wrench for a whole crew of merry men! (Incidentally, it may be asked on the side as a matter of academic interest if anyone here ever heard the driver of a combine singing and laughing at his work?) Masters of that now-forgotten art were relatively scarce and enjoyed considerable prestige. And truly it was something to see a perfectly symmetrical round stack of bundles, butts out to the weather, with all neatly and effectively topped off against rain and snow.

My Uncle was threshing out of the shock, and the job would take two or three days. Two wagons, furnished with hayracks, would collect the bundles from the shocks and haul them to the thresher. There would be two men to the wagon, one pitching bundles from the ground and handling the team, and the other "building" the load so that it would not slide off. The two haulers shared in pitching bundles to the separator.

Horsepower rigs were still in fashion, although steam was slowly coming in. Some of us still strongly favored horses, and we had reasons. The danger of straw stacks catching fire from flying sparks could scarcely be denied. And anyway, what was wrong with a cheap source of power that needed little tinkering and was always ready to go at a crack of the whip? One of these days they'd be putting engines on binders too, and then think of sparks flying over a dry grainfield on a windy day! Improvements were all right and fine; but there was a limit. When a man hitched four husky teams to the ends of "them there sweeps," cracked his whip and yelled "Git up," he sure had a helluva lot of power to play with!

And indeed he had! Even at my advanced age, when men are making trips to the moon, I still lean toward the horses, although I am fresh out of reasons.

And it *was* clever—the way they did it! Maybe you don't know. Well, a rig, like a giant coffee grinder, was firmly staked to the ground. Four or more sweeps extended about ten feet from the turning center of the rig. At the end of each sweep, a team was hitched, with guide lines connecting each horse's bit with the sweep ahead. The turning center was geared to a tumbling rod which was fitted with universal joints to compensate for the irregularities in the rod's position on its way to the separator with its horse-generated power. A stationary platform in the center of the rig gave the driver with his long whip a clear view of his teams. A member of the crew hovered handily around the circle of horses, on the off chance that one might develop far-out left-wing notions and start trouble. I never knew of a general strike, with direct action, among the power teams; but if one ever occurred, I'm sorry to regret that I wasn't there to see it!

44

It was late afternoon when the long-awaited threshers finally pulled in to our place—a not unimpressive procession. First came a buckboard drawn by a spanking team and carrying old Captain Bill Seton, owner and skipper of the outfit, along with his mechanic. (One noted casually that "Cap" required most of the buckboard seat.) Next came the lumbering, low-wheeled separator, big as a small house and a clumsy load for the four-horse team. After these were three wagons loaded with parts of the disassembled power rig: stakes, sweeps, gears, tumbling rod (itself a fair load), and various tools. The wagon would be available for hauling the wheat to market.

No time was wasted by the crew in getting everything shipshape for an early start next day. Evidently they all knew the one way to do this or that and the only acceptable order for the doing of it. There was a jaunty, even cocky, air about the way they approached their business. It was clear that they liked their work; and if (very rarely, mind you) one accompanied the rhythmic swing of his sledge hammer with a snatch of bawdy song, I would be the very last even to mention such a fact. But I *do* recall a passionate ditty in which a tender and sensitive lover declared his eternal constancy:

> And may I be hit
> With a bucket of mud,
> If ever I cease to love!

I remember that I was convulsed with mirth by the precision with which the sledge-hammer blow coincided with the sloppy impact of the bucket on the faithless lover!

—But, then, I was only a mischievous boy at the time.

The threshing crew completed its arrangements by dark; and after bathing hilariously at the horse trough by sloshing buckets of cold well water on each other, they went to bed down by the new haystacks near the barn.

We were using our straw to make winter shelters that could double as fodder, come deep snows after Christmas. My Uncle had built rude frameworks of poles cut in the wooded bottoms of the creek, and on these the thresher elevator would dump the straw to be spread and arranged by a stacker with a pitchfork—the dirtiest man on the job and the least contented. You never heard him singing up there in the dust, and the position frequently changed incumbents.

We were all up and around at the first streak of daylight and were through with breakfast before sunup. The neighbors were beginning to arrive; and one of the haulers, having loaded the day before, was already on hand with a rackful of bundles drawn up on the right side of the feeder's table. Next to him would be the band cutter, who would receive the bundles pitched from the wagon, slash their twine bands, and push the loosened stalks to his left, heads toward the machine. There the feeder would ease the grain into the separator's mouth and against a whirling spike-tooth drum. Incidentally, he would be at pains not to lose some of his hands in the operation.

45

Now the power teams are being hitched to the four sweeps. The horses, feeling the excitement in the air, chew their bits, rattle their harnesses, and paw.

One of the wagons that will haul the grain to the elevator in town is waiting yonder under the machine's grain spout. The feeder and band cutter are taking their places. The driver has climbed onto his stationary control platform, and the machinist has finished his oiling.

There we are in a breathless hush of time, all set to go, waiting only the word from the skipper of the outfit, old Captain Bill Seton. He has some last-minute inspections to make, and the horses can wait while we have a look at old Bill. They will have plenty of pawing to do before this day, and the next, are over!

46

In the first place, as I later learned, Bill was called "old" less as a biological observation than by way of recognizing him as a legendary figure among his contemporaries. He could hardly have been more than sixty at that time—a ruddy-faced, full-blown "stout" man in the old generous meaning of the term. The brass rings in his ears might have betokened strange, romantic doings in some South Sea paradise. He wore them unself-consciously, and no one ventured to inquire.

He had a barrel chest and a voice box to go with it. When Bill let go in a full-lunged sea chanty, it was said, loose things shook and rattled. A jolly man himself, Bill was often quoted with chuckles. It seems he was especially gifted in the coining of ingenious cuss words, and this at a time when distinguished practitioners of that lost art still actively indulged in "cussing contests." These affairs were held with no sacrilegious intent, but merely as innocent entertainment—"good clean fun," as the saying goes. The idea was to outdo one's adversary in the sustained utterance of original epithets and imprecations fit only for the ears of a mule.

It is only as a conscientious historian that I have mentioned this barbaric sport of a bygone era; and indeed I have had access to the best sources. For instance, I once carried the hod for a plasterer who had achieved championship rating in his practice of the now lost art. I myself heard him declaim luridly and without hesitation or repetition for a solid half hour. His peroration, preserved for posterity among my archives, is strictly "classified."

Whether Bill was ever a captain in fact, no one knew or greatly cared. No doubt he had spent much of his boyhood, youth, and early manhood on British vessels in the days of sail, and he well might have won the title. Perhaps when, at last, he found himself becalmed in the mid-continent doldrums, he took up threshing as the nearest thing to being skipper on a tramp ship that our Plains had to offer. Much of his remuneration must have been imaginary. Certainly he wasn't getting rich. None of his breed ever did, I heard. According to rumor, most of them lost their rigs — and their shirts.

47

Surely by now the cagey power teams have been pawing long enough. The great moment has arrived. The captain fills his lungs and bawls the command:

Let — 'er — ro-o-oll, boys!

Let — 'er — ro-o-o-ll!

The driver on his platform yells at his horses and cracks his long whip over their bobbing rumps. They squat and lean against their collars, switch their tails, and buck against the heavy drag until they get the flywheel spinning. The rig begins a throaty rattle that deepens into a muffled roar as the wheat stalks fill the hungry belly.

We are off and rolling!

And look at that golden stream beginning to pour into the wagon! Thick as a man's arm — well, almost. The corn crop is gone — not even fit for fodder; and it hasn't rained a drop since that gully-washer — when was it? Sometime in the spring. But wheat was mostly made before the drouth got bad, and it looks like something to sing about.

93

Old Bill is bellowing an old chanty above the uproar, and his crew jokingly swells the roaring refrain:

> There was an old skipper, I don't know his name,
>   'Way! Hey! Blow the man down!
> Although he once played a remarkable game,
>   Give me some time to blow the man down.
>
> His ship lay becalmed in the tropical seas,
>   'Way! Hey! Blow the man down!
> He whistled all day, but in vain, for a breeze,
>   Give me some time to blow the man down.
>
> A seal heard the whistle and loudly did call,
>   'Way! Hey! Blow the man down!
> 'Roll up your white canvas, jib, spanker, and all,
>   Give me some time to blow the man down.'
>
> Then the breeze it blew gaily, a terrible gale,
>   'Way! Hey! Blow the man down!
> And the ship flew along with nary a sail,
>   Give me some time to blow the man down.

The horses seem to like the song, pricking their ears and trying to hurry a bit.

The captain, having completely "blown the man down," finally takes another tack, singing like the homesick sailor he probably often is. (And what a voice to vie with the raucous bass of the separator!)

> For it's home, dearest home—it's home I want to be,
> Our topsails are hoisted, and we'll away to sea;
> O, the oak and the ash and the bonnie birchen tree
> They're all growing green in the old countrie.
>
> And if it be a girl, she shall wear a gold ring;
> And if it be a boy, he must fight for his king—
> With a silver-spangled buckle and a jacket trimmed
>   in blue,
> And walk quarter-deck like his daddy used to do.

That one, especially, got into where I live. I learned all of it, words and air, later on when I came to know the captain well. It suggested a sad, sweet story I liked to tell myself when I whistled or hummed the quaint, homesick tune. I could see the sailor boy in a British ship far from dear old England — in the tropics, likely, judging by the trees remembered in his "own countrie." He is thinking of a lonely girl who is waiting yonder far over the seas — waiting and waiting. There is going to be a baby that its daddy may never see. So it's home, dearest home, and it's home he ought to be — home, dearest home, in his own countrie — with the oak and the ash — and the girl — and the baby.

I lived to know the captain when I was no longer a boy, and when no one ever called him "old" any more — just "Captain." He used to limp three-legged into the office where I worked; and when it happened that we were alone together there, he sang to me in a low, husky voice, pausing often to "get his wind."

There was an interminable chanty that amounted to a personally conducted voyage around the jolly old world, touching at all important ports. I believe it covered the Seven Seas; but, after a stormy eastward crossing of the Atlantic, we didn't get beyond the Canaries. The captain had been having special trouble with his breathing for some time — "Nothing serious," mind you, "just uncomfortable, like."

That day, I remember, he was proceeding with his lyrical voyage around the globe and making rather heavy weather of it. He had just sung the line "And when we came to Tenerife" when his voice failed him, and he fell to panting violently, fighting for breath like a drowning man.

He sang no more that day; and I never heard what happened at Tenerife. But I know what happened to my old friend. I could repeat the highly sophisticated Greek name for the trouble he had, and I could even spell it successfully. But I will do neither here. It's no way for a good man to die, by God! So I prefer to fancy that some injury of his heroic youth had resulted at last in his taking off — just when he became too old to sing.

48

But—

A few moments ago—or maybe a lifetime—all of us, men, horses, and a boy, were happily threshing wheat out of the shock, when the captain, remembering his youth, began blowing men down. Now we have been blown far across the seas by a high wind of song—even unto Tenerife, where voices cease and the long forgetting begins.

It's like a tableau back yonder, waiting only for a booming voice (*Let—'er—r-o-o-ll!*) to break out suddenly into action: The driver on his platform, his long whiplash curled motionless in the air; the eight horses leaning to their lathered collars; a bundle just leaving the pitchfork of the hauler, almost in the arms of the band cutter with his knife aloft; the stacker like a clowning ghost up there in a still cloud of dust and straw; the deep, enchanted silence of the separator, needing only a flick of the whiplash to be loud.

But perhaps it's only getting noon forever there, with dinner waiting in the quiet house.

There should be boisterous larking at the horse trough when the boys are washing up. The pulley at the open well should be whining at the burden of the bucket. The sleeping house should waken soon with scrambled talk and laughter.

The improvised dining table in the sitting room must still be waiting, heavy with a feast whose menu, merely spoken, would be song. Good women have been working there for days to get that dinner, each giving of her special best in jolly competition.

The biscuits must be getting cold by now. Is no one ever hungry any more?

A few years ago, when young people had just begun to take my arm at stairways and street crossings, I made a sentimental journey to the farm.

A grove of sapling cottonwoods had grown enormously and out of all proportion to good sense. The house was still where it belonged, though richly ruined by improvements. There were no strawstacks or straw-roofed sheds, and the barns were strange. The horse trough and the well had vanished, but there could be no doubt at all about where they had been.

I was standing with the current grandpa of the place in the middle of the driveway, now paved with gravel, beaten hard.

"Right here," I said, "there used to be a fine old open well. What ever happened to it? Do you know?"

The old man shook his head slowly, fixed me with a quizzical, dubious look, and said:

"Ain't ever been a well here, mister!"

49

It rained!

After all those dusty months of 1894, it rained. It should have been dramatic, but it wasn't. There was no great wind; there was no thunder, no lightning. The sky just grew overcast at twilight, and the dark came in with a casual drizzle that increased to a sighing, nightlong drench.

It was good for the pastures and the fall plowing; but it was more than rain for me. As I look back, I can see that it was like a great curtain falling between me and boyhood—a transparent gauze curtain, but impenetrable. I never quite got back to the farm again in the old way.

A week later I began bell ringing at the little college on the hill.

I had no way of keeping time, so Professor Pile loaned me an old key-wind Waltham watch. Its outsize silver case (made when silver was cheap) reminded me pleasantly of a certain flattish, mildly flavored turnip that I preferred to all others in a patch. Being an antique, it properly exemplified the ancient virtue of integrity. If it told you the time was so and so, thereupon you knew it was precisely that in every nook and corner of the time zone. Also its burly presence was reassuring, and whenever I pulled it out for consultation, all observers realized that the horological situation was well in hand.

At first, time seemed a treacherous thing, ever ready to take mean advantage of my slightest inattention to the crawling minute hand. At such times it would become, all of a sudden, much later than it had any reasonable right to be. But after a few weeks I began to note an uncanny rapport between the Waltham and me. More and more, my spontaneous guesses at the time coincided with the watch's expert testimony, until I no longer needed to consult it more than once before the critical moment arrived.

50

I lived about a mile and a half from the college and, regardless of the weather, I was obliged to be in my tower room, pulling the bell rope, at exactly 6:30 A.M. That awakened the institution and set the cooks to work. During the long days of spring and fall, this duty was a pleasure rather than a hardship. But after the holidays, when the temperature often dropped to thirty below zero and sometimes forty, it required some stamina to head out into the biting dark. Even so, there was enchantment in the cold-hushed predawn world with me alone to feel it. Years later, when I was writing *The Song of the Messiah*, something of those still, clear, frozen mornings got into the lines:

> And nights were frozen bubbles on the strain,
> Blown vast with silence.

Then there were times when night was a howling chaos of snow, and dawn a blind white ghost of day without a sun. I remember especially such a blizzard morning when I should have stayed at home and left the bell in silence. I do not know just how I found my way to the college. So long as there were houses on the street, I caromed back and forth, thus approximating the direction of the road. But soon there were no more houses and nothing to use as a guide except the breathtaking northwest wind, whetted with frozen snow. That experience and various others of the sort later found their way into the blizzard on the Yellowstone in *The Song of Hugh Glass:*

Black blindness grew white blindness — and 'twas day. . . .
White blindness grew black blindness — and 'twas night. . . .

Early in my life I came to think of courage as the great Mother Virtue, and of endurance as its chief manifestation. The patterns that have dominated my life have supported this view, and long ago it was expressed in mottoes on my bookplate: "Don't be a quitter; stay and break even"; "I win by delays."

In later years, when I had accumulated some knowledge of Fortune's "slings and arrows," I was able to write, with deep conviction and a soul-freeing sense of acceptance: Learn to work with a joyous absence of hope.

John and I sometimes created absurd hardships by way of testing ourselves, like plodding all night on muddy roads in a pouring rain or walking forty-five miles without food or water.

That blizzard morning, as in other times of testing, there seemed to be two of me — the one who fought the storm, prevailing against it, and the other who observed the battle and was proud of me.

This is the theme of my *The Song of Hugh Glass:*

So sits the artist throned above his art . . .

The duty and the beauty of endeavor,
The privilege of going on forever,
A victor in the moment.

Finally somehow I fought my way through the wild blindness and found myself on the front steps of the college, amazed, half frozen, and out of breath. But I was there, and that is what mattered.

There were times in midwinter when the black evenings after my last bell were quite as bad as the stormy black mornings.

51

Shortly after my 6:30 bell, men students came tumbling down out of the fourth floor dormitory and through my tower room on the way to breakfast in the basement. A half hour later the first classes met. Thereafter the schedule was like an old song that monotonously sings itself: 7:50, 8:40, 9:30, 10:20, 11:10, 12:00 o'clock, noon; 1:00, 1:50, 2:40, 3:30, 4:20, 5:10, 6:00 o'clock, supper. Bells ten minutes apart marked the end of one class period and beginning of the next.

Our student body, certainly numbering less than fifty at first, was a motley assemblage indeed; but we were all in college, and properly impressed by the fact.

The chief entrance requirements of the old Nebraska Normal College seemed to be the applicant's conscious ignorance and his determination to do something about it. There were some whose education had been limited to occasional attendance at a country school in the dead of winter when there was nothing more important to do. Those were out to overtake fast-fleeing opportunity, and they were excellent students in general.

I remember especially a rather green farmhand about thirty years old who undoubtedly had grown weary of working for thirteen dollars per month and being nobody in particular. When he entered our college, considerable private tutoring was needed to prepare him for classwork. I lived to know him after he had gone far beyond our N.N.C. and become a distinguished educator.

Incidentally, he married the lady who had been his tutor in simple arithmetic. She was also my first Latin teacher and like an elder sister to me. It was all in the family, so to speak, and on occasion I still tell the story with pride, as you see. I saw the noble lady when she was nearing her hundredth birthday. The way she leaned to me and whispered in my ear, she might have been sharing a guilty secret with a trusted partner in sin. "Oh, John," she said, "really, I'm ninety-nine!"

It seemed at least a misdemeanor, if not quite a felony.

52

As for my own case, it was as though the little college had been created for me. It released me from the listless boredom I had come to feel in school and lifted me to a higher, creative level of being. Often there came upon me a thrilled sense of expectancy, as though something particularly glorious were getting ready to happen all at once. I would try to think what made me feel so, but reasons seemed not to apply. It was simply "in the air" of the world, and I think it radiated from J. M. Pile.

I would mistrust my glowing image of the man had I not known many of his old students over the years. It has been a long while now since I met the last of these, but I recall that it was the same with all of them. There would be the usual routine reminiscence with, perhaps, a touch of "old grad" jollity. But when Pile was mentioned, the mood of the meeting would change, and one might have gathered from the ensuing conversation that all of us had seen the same revealing light.

Curious students of history must have noted how, occasionally, by the accidents of time and place, some man of quite ordinary gifts may be caught up in a dynamic social pattern too big for him. Instead of being eliminated by the discrepancy, he may be reshaped and fitted to the pattern by the mythmaking faculty of men, and come to be regarded as a "great man," or he may even become a folk hero, jealously protected against sacrilegious questioning. In such cases it is not the man but the myth that is cherished — the amber, and not the fly. There must be many cases also in which, for lack of the amber, the fly is lost.

As I look back upon Pile now, it seems clear that he was essentially a great man caught in a pattern far too small for him. In those days, naturally enough, we took him pretty much for granted. Of course he was more remarkable than other men we knew. He was "Pile."

We all knew he was a whiz in mathematics, for once a week he gave the chapel period to mental arithmetic. In this class of the whole, he taught us how to solve problems "in our heads." His purpose was to develop the power of attention and clarity of thought. Attendance was required, but compulsion was unnecessary. Just to be present was a fascinating adventure, and everyone was engaged in it shortly after the class assembled. You had to be so engaged, for if your mind wandered from the matter under consideration, you would almost certainly have an embarrassing question thrown at you in a sweetly sympathetic voice. It was uncanny. He seemed to read your thoughts, if any! But when your whole attention was given to the problem, even when you came up with the wrong answer, it was as though the man purred like a happy cat that has just swallowed a mouse. The unusual breadth across his brows, together with flourishing sideburns, enhanced the look of feline satisfaction.

Once, several of us who were studying advanced algebra ran across a problem somewhere that was supposed to be a regular hellion, even for the experts. It was certainly beyond us. So we decided to try it on Pile just to see what he would do about it. Like diligent pupils humbly in need of teacher's help, we presented the problem. He looked at it awhile, and then said *hm-m-m*. Going to the blackboard, he wrote some symbols, stroked his chin, and said *hm-m-m* again. Then he wrote some more symbols, stroked his chin in silence for a while, and finally with a flourish wrote the answer. "There you are!" he said. And indeed we were, and properly impressed, for we knew enough to know there had been a lot of plain and fancy factoring between those cryptic remarks and strokings of the chin.

53

I know now that Pile must have had a most remarkable understanding of world affairs — and that before the airplane made the planet small, before the advent of news analysts, radios, and television. One chapel period each week was devoted to current events. The man was far ahead of his day. As early as 1896, when I completed the Professional Teachers Course, he discussed the position of imperial Germany in Central Europe, pointing out the danger involved in the situation — a dynamic nation, hemmed in by powerful competitors and needing to expand. I remember his saying something about a water kettle on a hot stove with the lid soldered on. We laughed about it then.

Also I remember a prophetic statement he made about the same time. "You young people," he said, "should live to see the day when the two dominant nations of the world will be the United States and Russia." This was before the Spanish-American War, and the United States had not yet become a world power. It was at least twenty years before the Czar was overthrown by the Bolshevik Revolution, and Russia was still a backward nation, dreaming the old medieval dream; and the British Empire was still in its heyday, mistress of the Seven Seas.

It must be noted that Pile was not always forward-looking. In the matter of grammar, for instance, he was definitely "dated," as seen from our dizzy height of time. He might even be pronounced Victorian, although one hesitates to employ an epithet so harsh. In any case, he failed to foresee the day when English grammar would become obsolete, according to advanced educators then yet unborn. He seems to have been a congenital grammarian; and to his dying day he nursed the belief that a working knowledge of one's language and its structure was of importance to the literate. It is to be doubted that he ever considered the possible practicality of absorbing such knowledge through the pores, without conscious effort.

Grammar was a required subject in our college, and no one escaped it. Furthermore, no one was encouraged to take mathematics and grammar at the same time. As already noted, for several years I had been experimenting with verse, striving to make words sing while they were saying; and I was fascinated by this formal study of verbal mechanics. It was definitely "up my alley," and I wasted no time in making it my own.

My wholehearted conversion to the gospel according to Pile must have been conspicuous, for soon I was being used somewhat as a gadfly for the class. "Johnny, jump up and tell them!" he would say when some question had searched the back seats in vain for an answer. It was embarrassing, but it was effective; and since I was by far the smallest and youngest, no one ever seemed to resent my enforced priggery.

I did not soon escape this extra service to my benefactor. "What are you taking this term, Johnny?" he would ask. I would tell him. "—And grammar of course," he would add. "But, Professor, I've taken it twice!" "Take it again." And so I did, brazenly on my front seat.

54

I did escape eventually—into the august world of Latin grammar!

It was with no larcenous intent that I decided to "take" Latin. My attitude certainly was not covetous. I took it simply because that was considered the thing to do in those days. Youngsters were expected to take Latin in keeping with a prevalent conviction that it was indispensable in the process of education. Not until at least a half-century later did dangerously "advanced" educators begin to ask what the hell the vocative of *mensa* or even the pluperfect of *amo* could possibly have to do with the price of eggs.

But I liked my teacher, Miss Anna Byrne. I liked her so much that soon I was proficient even unto the third and fourth declensions; and to conjugate *amo* for her became a heady delight. She had only to express a yearning for the principal parts of an irregular verb, and she had them forthwith; for I could warble all that glorious stuff like a canary.

And then!

The Gallic Wars and the tramp of Caesar's legions! The gleaming cohorts flowing in rivers of spears! And the splendor that was Rome!

So I was on the great highway of time at last, with all the enchanted classical world ahead of me, and mighty Vergil like a towering peak in the far offing yonder.

55

With the beginning of my second year at the college, one Fräulein Emma Klintwort, fresh from the old country across the sea, appeared on our campus as student of English and teacher of German.

There were no takers for her offering that first term, excepting only myself. The language of Goethe and Heine, somewhat damaged by vulgar usage, was not only without honor in our community of unreconstructed peasantry, but even carried comical overtones for superior American ears. I myself, for all my pride of ancestry, had been unaware of any commanding need for the tongue — before I encountered the Fräulein face to face.

She was in the full bloom of twenty at the time (and I do mean *bloom*), while I had only lately turned sixteen. Her hair looked like molasses taffy overpulled. Her eyes —

Discerning students of this faithful history may (or may not) have noted my repugnance for the sentimental; and now that I am grown very old, and accordingly very wise, let us hope, I really should not be telling this at all. But it's simply the God's truth, and what's wrong with that? Anyway, I have not forgotten how something joyously troubling happened to me then — something only casually related to linguistics. So I enrolled.

Our class of one met twice a week — on Wednesdays and Saturdays. I think I never studied so hard before or since in all my life; and the Fräulein pronounced my progress phenomenal — or sounds to that effect in her enchanting experimental English.

Classwork, I gather from shards of memory, was largely ecstasy. After paying due deference to the grammatical mysteries, we usually adjourned into a committee of the whole, wherein the Fräulein recited German lyrics, explaining and repeating until they came forth singing for me with their burdens of joy and sorrow, love and loss.

There were times, I am sure, when I must have heard more melody than meaning, what with watching the way her lips managed the umlauts, and how her rolling *r*'s rippled out of her pretty white throat.

Sometimes on homesick days, in lieu of the lyrics, she would talk of her girlhood and her home in Glückstadt an der Elbe. Glückstadt, city of happiness! What a place to be from and go back to!

She did go back that spring, and never returned to us.
Well — I learned about German from her, which I thought
I'd just mention in passing.

56

It was not long before I began to have additional private
classes in Latin and in mathematics. If I was ready for a subject and there were no other takers, then I went ahead alone.
In advanced Latin Professor Conn was my mentor. Under
his tutelage I read all of the *Commentaries,* most of Cicero, and
much of Tacitus before we tackled Horace on the way to
the *Aeneid,* which I was reading for pleasure at fifteen.

Professor Conn never assigned lessons to me. "Well, go
ahead," he would say, perhaps after an illuminating talk
about our reading. Usually I spent five hours a day — from
1:00 P.M. to 6:00 — in preparation for our next meeting. All
my other studying was crowded into the forenoons with occasional work at night. Recitation was a simple matter — I
reading, he interrupting me now and then to ask about some
grammatical construction. Gradually we became less like
boy and man or student and teacher, and more like friends,
happily sharing a rich experience.

He was undoubtedly master of his subject, and I think the
boy's eager interest amused and delighted him. I recall a look
he sometimes had, as though he were busy keeping serious,
and I remember with an overwhelming affection the time
when a fit of boisterous laughter briefly united the tall,
stately man and the little boy in ageless companionship. It
was when "pious Aeneas" was about to descend into Avernus,
there to behold the tragic face of Dido rising like a moon
through the boughs. (My God, *what* a line!) I do not have my
library at hand, and that was seventy-five years ago. The old
man's memory may well be less than perfect, but I do recall
something about a sibyl and the entrance to the nether world.

Also there was something about a sow nursing thirty pigs.

I was reading at sight, rather breathlessly, and failed to note the gender of the noun for "pig." Pigs in classical literature, according to my experience, were mostly hunted boars; and so, in my hasty construction, a boar was discovered *flagrante delicto,* suckling a litter of thirty!

Conn exploded. I followed, laughing the harder to see him laugh; for his ears seemed to fold back like a mule's, and he brayed.

57

Years later Conn became president of the fine institution which grew out of the little pioneer school; and it was said that he never missed the opportunity, when we happened to be present together at some public function, to tell of our Latin adventures in the good old days. "Johnny never knew," he would declare, with some affectionate latitude, we may suppose, "how often I stayed up after midnight, trying to keep up with him, for I fear my Latin had become a trifle rusty from disuse."

When he was almost old and I was getting to be a little less than young, I came to realize how very much I loved him long ago and loved him still. The realization came with a glorifying experience that is still a mystery to me, and I tell it here for what it may be worth to any curious reader.

It was in 1935. Conn was retiring and the college was celebrating his silver anniversary as president. It was going to be a big affair. Old students from all over the nation were to be present, and a bevy of dignitaries, including His Excellency, the Governor, would be on hand to grace the occasion.

My Mona and I were there as guests of the Conns; and I was free of care, for, at my insistence, I would not be asked to speak. I did not want to make a speech. There was much too much to say.

But word came on the eve of the event that the Governor could not come. A streetcar strike had broken out in Omaha, and he was needed there. "So I guess, John," Conn said, "you will have to make the Governor's speech."

I was scared, for, as I told my Mona, I hadn't the slightest notion of what to say, there was so much. She told me not to worry, I'd be all right after a good night's sleep. But I worried more or less all night. In the morning my mind seemed as empty as a paper sack, and I was still scared. What in the world was I to do? People would expect me to do well, for there had been some talk of me. The whole beautiful, wooded campus, vibrantly alive with its P.A. system, would be eagerly expectant.

Then relief came. We were eating a picnic dinner out under the trees when word came to me that the strike was over and the Governor would be present with his blessed speech after all!

How I enjoyed that dinner! — until news came about two o'clock that the strike was on again and the Governor had returned to Omaha. I felt sick and resentful.

"Walk up and down out yonder in the trees and smoke," my Mona advised me, "and it will all come to you."

I walked and smoked, but nothing happened. So I walked and smoked some more. Still nothing happened. The show would begin at two thirty, and it was already past two!

Now the people took their seats on the shady hillside, fusing into a happily murmuring crowd. Distinguished alumni and the bevy of dignitaries (lacking the Governor, alas!) were stiffly planted on their hard chairs. From my torture seat I viewed the entire assemblage eagerly waiting — for the fiasco to begin!

A boatman drifting without oars, feeling the suck of mighty waters just before the plunge into the cataract, might feel somewhat as I was feeling.

Straight ahead of me some fifteen or twenty paces away sat my faithful Mona, radiant with expectation. Her face glowed like an incandescent light. Evidently she was convinced that this was going to be a positive and memorable wow, whereas

I *knew* it was going to be a dismal flop. I shook my head at her and frowned; but her face seemed unshakable, and the glow increased. I had often seen that illuminated countenance shining out of my audience, and it had always given me strength; but now it mocked me. Shamed by the glory in her face, I braced myself against my fear. I'd do my damnedest, but what the hell was I going to say?

The introductions and the little talks of the distinguished grads began. Only they were not all little talks. Evidently there had been some misunderstanding about the invitation to "say a few words." The talks ran on and on. The seats grew harder and harder. Backs grew stiffer and stiffer.

Finally my Uncle, Charles L. Culler, a well-known schoolman, arose stiffly at the calling of his name, and in lieu of a speech told his audience a little story.

This young lover, it seems, had for several hours been holding his ample sweetheart on his lap, when the young lady inquired tenderly, "Darling, are you getting tired?" Whereupon the young man replied, "I was tired an hour or two ago, sweetheart, but now I'm paralyzed!"

The hillside roared with laughter, and my Uncle got no further with his talk; but after that the speeches were notably shorter.

Then, at long last, the dreaded "moment of truth" arrived. Conn arose and went to the microphone, screwing it up to accommodate his six feet two. I tried not to hear what he was saying, for I knew it was all about me, and all I had to give were some perfunctory words and a heartache. At length he turned to me and spoke my name slowly. The audience responded, a bit more than politely, perhaps. Then the whole hillside went ominously still, as with the ceasing of a great breath.

I started across the platform, bitter-hearted and afraid; but about the center of the stage something happened in my chest. It was not unlike a runner's second wind. I had felt it once before when John and I were testing our endurance on a five-mile course. It happened in the third mile, I think.

The overtaxed lungs seemed to flop and turn over, leaving a cool, spacious cavity and a thrill of well-being.

While I was screwing the microphone down to accommodate my five feet two, I looked out across the crowd—faces and faces and faces, and each of them and all of them were inexpressibly dear! A wave of love swept through me, and there was a throbbing of blocked tears behind my eyes. Then I heard myself speaking: "In the beginning was the Word, and the Word was God. And God said, 'Let there be light'— and there *was* light!"

I had not known that I would begin so, and I had no thought of what I would say next. Several times during my troubled teens I had experienced the ecstasy of sleepwalking; and there was the same profound peace and selfless enlargement of being. I could feel rather than hear the smooth flow of fusing words and shapen phrases, without conscious concern for their meaning. They felt good in my throat and, although they were somehow mine, I did not seem to make or guide them.

It was with no sense of elapsed time that I again became clearly aware of the place and circumstances.

All across the hillside the audience was standing in silence.

There was no applause.

My Mona told me that I had spoken for twelve or fifteen minutes, apparently without effort. She could not recall much of what she had heard. It was all about bringing the light of learning to the frontier—and Conn; and it was less like a speech, she said, than a poem becoming a prayer. What impressed her most was the flow of "cadenced phrasing— smooth as the bend of a bird's wing," she remarked. "There was no peroration. The voice just flowed into silence."

58

At the beginning of my second term after entering college, I enrolled in the Professional Teachers Course. Graduates were entitled to a second-grade county teacher's certificate, which became first-grade after a term of satisfactory school-room experience. The college offered only two courses, the other being the Advanced Scientific Course, leading to a B.S. degree, normally after two more years.

Although I spent a greatly disproportionate share of my study time on Latin, my general progress was rapid, owing largely to the private-class arrangement made for me. Superficially it might seem that my educational opportunities were meager, but, as a matter of fact, I enjoyed the benefits of an enlightened system fifty years or more before its time. It was our very limitations that made this possible and necessary.

As I dream back into the mood of that time, I do not remember ever having worked unpleasantly hard on my studies. It was all more like beckoning adventure than demanding duty; and I might have been a rich boy with friendly tutors to share encounters with the new and strange.

Thus I was made at least aware of English literature, its vast scope and grandeur, some years before I was ready for it, according to the rules. The course was offered by my first Latin teacher, Miss Byrne, and the text she chose was Taine's monumental work. Of all things! It was no wonder that the small handful of perplexed entrants dwindled quickly to one. It was curiosity that held me. What might be lurking yonder in that mysterious and apparently impenetrable forest of words!

Probably because of our comradeship in the love of Latin, Miss Byrne was willing to remain with me. By this time she was boarding in our home, and I had the advantage of being near her. Several times a week we met with Taine, I reading, she interpreting. Much went over my head, I know, but I grew in the vital atmosphere the book created; and if my general conception of English literature thus acquired was like a far-flung landscape transparently veiled in a gauze of fog, there were, nevertheless, giants in the land, standing tall and still against a changeless sky.

I completed the Teachers Course in May 1896, at the age of fifteen. There were some twenty of us in the class and I was, by far, the youngest and smallest of the lot, a little boy among adults, according to our graduation picture that I still hoard among my cherished trifles. There are impressive mustaches in that picture, and the ladies, safely clothed from chin to instep against a probably prurient world, are definitely grown up and already, in proper mien and poise, quite the teachers they are soon to be.

That summer I taught an advanced Cicero class for Conn, who was lecturing on pedagogy to various county "teachers' institutes." My students were mostly veteran teachers, validating their certificates by attending summer school. That must have been something of a side show, but Cicero was one of my old friends, and verily we got results. I'm sure I was more Connishly professorial than Conn himself; but I was treated with respect, not unmixed, we may assume, with amusement and affection.

My face still burns when I recall a high point in that summer's experience. We were hearing the great orator proclaim what a consummate heel this treacherous, dissolute Cataline really was. "O war to be feared," he cried, "since Cataline will have a bodyguard of *scortorum!*"

Clearly, the text said *scortorum,* the genitive plural of *scortus;* but the modest young lady who was reading at the time resorted to euphemistical pussyfooting—"a bodyguard of [long hesitation]—a bodyguard of *immoral women!*" she faltered weakly.

"No, no!" I said. "This is a great orator speaking. Please give us the correct wording." And she did so, blushing violently, while the class snickered.

I really needed a good spanking!

59

At the time of my graduation from the Teachers Course I had been working at intervals for at least a year on what was to be my magnum opus — *The Divine Enchantment.* I have already considered it somewhat in this history, along with certain collateral doings of my Early Tombstone period. As wakeful readers will remember, I had already sacrificed much tentative literature to the cleansing flames, and thus I was purified for the final all-out effort to justify my brief existence.

Brief?

As I write, that was seventy-five years ago! But I was far from being a morbid youngster. There were two of me; and at an early age one knew well the heady wine of life.

But slyly worded ads, addressed to pubescent youth, were appearing in many papers of the day, and these convinced both John and me that, sooner or later (most probably much sooner, alas!), we would begin to waste away to an early demise. Verily we had the symptoms, according to the ads, but quite as verily we lacked the required five dollars. And how could we ever tell our parents about the frightful situation?

John faced doom with his usual grin, like the hero that he was, while I toiled to give something worthy to the world before I should be gathered to my fathers. Often I wakened in the night to light my little coal-oil lamp and work awhile in the enchanted silence of the sleeping house. And as I went about in daytime, serving the lesser will, unfinished lines and ghosts of images haunted and troubled me.

All this while, as throughout much of my life, I was greatly concerned with the problem of living successfully in a world of people, most of whom outtopped my five feet two. Since the continuous, compelling need to find a working answer has been a determining factor in my life, I must take note of it here before going further with this history.

In matters of the mind, I seemed to have small cause for worry; but that was not enough for either my world or me. I needed to be even a little better in matters of the body too. So before I reached my teens I had begun training. I could not add one jot or tittle to my stature by taking thought; but, by God, I could be stronger, faster, abler than the average, if I put my mind to it. "Mere shank bones," I used to tell myself consolingly, "can be had at a nickel a pound from any butcher!"

The memory of my Father was reassuring—only an inch or two taller than I, but fashioned like a giant. Why, he could hold more at arm's length than any other man in the Kansas City streetcar system! I remembered when he stripped to swim—the full chest, the ropy, slender waist, the muscles on his back like eggs in a basket! Maybe I could come to be almost like that!

The determined and unceasing effort to excel physically paid off well; and I beg my generous readers to be lenient if I seem to boast in recounting my youthful achievements. So help me God! it's nothing of the sort, and I am too keenly aware of half-empty muscle sacks and wrinkled skin to take much pleasure in remembering the way it used to be. Be kind, be kind.

By my twentieth year, then, I could lift my weight, one hundred and twenty pounds, from the floor over my head with one arm. I could tear a pack of playing cards in two with my hands. I had a chest expansion of ten inches, compared with an average of about three for husky men. One stunt of which I was especially proud was performed thus: Filling my oversize lungs and expanding the muscles of chest, underarm, and back, I would have the tape tied snugly about me. Then, deflating the lungs and shrinking the muscles, I could pass a plug hat under the tape. It was an act I had seen in a side show.

In addition to calisthenic training, I spent much time with the punching bag, and developed a wallop that gave me the high score on the striking machine for our county—1705 against averages of seven and eight hundred. I had a system. Being light, I needed speed to get momentum; so, briskly approaching the padded target, I'd leap forward and deliver a short-arm jab when the hurled body weight was still in the air. The momentum of the body and the sharp smack of the short-arm punch, neatly synchronized, did the trick. The recording needle leaped about the dial!

While at my peak in such practices, I worked for some months as reporter on the *Sioux City Tribune*. One day I dropped in at a hangout where sporting men congregated. There was excited talk about betting odds and horses with fanciful names. There were jockeys, delightfully smaller men than I, who swaggered about importantly. A striking machine just like ours in the pool hall back home caught my eye when a light-footed middle-size man with a broken nose and cauliflower ears danced up on his toes, took off his coat, and swung viciously at the target. *Wham!* The needle registered 1100.

Thinking there must be something wrong with the machine, I waited until the space about it was cleared; then I stripped my coat and did my stunt. *Smack!* The co-ordination was perfect. The needle leaped to 1700.

I was putting on my coat when a man in a checkered suit and a loud shirt with a diamond-studded tie tapped me on the shoulder.

Excuse him; but he wanted to know where I got that wallop and what I was planning to do with it.

Had any fights?

No fights. I was a natural-born pacifist, and I heard fighting was hard on the eyes. Why did he ask?

Well, training fighters for the prize ring was his business, and if I'd come and train with him, he'd make me world champion of my class within a year!

He followed me about with eager arguments.

Why, it was a cinch! Nothing to it! Them bantamweights couldn't hurt me; and when I landed with my ton of brick—!

What ever was the matter with me?

Did I hate money?
Sometimes I think of that man, and I wonder.

60

Although after graduation from the Teachers Course I was legally eligible to teach a country school, I was clearly too young as well as a trifle undersize. So it seemed advisable for me to complete the Advanced Scientific Course before applying for a school.

I was ahead of the course when I enrolled, and thus I was able to find much free time for *The Divine Enchantment*. It was completed early in 1898 when I had just turned seventeen. At the end of the term, and of the course, the definitive version of the little book was all neatly written out and painstakingly bound in buckram, ready for the test of "Fortune and men's eyes."

It was glorious to be alive!

But as I look back over my years it seems somehow that I was never allowed for long to be completely and joyously triumphant over any achievement or success. Always a shadow fell across the glory; and it was not without meaning that I wrote in "The Ghostly Brother," reminiscent of my boyhood dream:

> When the world is cherished most,
> You shall hear my haunting cry,
> See me rising like a ghost.

A great dream had come true, and I had lived to see it!

I had completed the Scientific Course with high grades. But where was I to find four dollars to pay for my diploma? That was quite some money for us in those days. I could not get it from my Mother with her occasional work at a dollar a day. I could not force myself to go to Pile and confess the shameful lack. No doubt he would have been glad to waive payment of the fee, but I lacked the face to tell him.

So I did not appear for graduation. Instead, I was pulling weeds in a big potato field at seventy-five cents a day.

I once saw a photograph of my graduating class receiving his diploma and degree, for there was only one of him—all dignified importance, a handle-bar mustache, and a four-dollar smile of satisfaction!

Yet I was not for pity. In one pocket of my coat I carried Tennyson's selected lyrics, and in the other, Browning's. It was as though they cast a spell of invulnerability about me. And in the darkest moments, with painful wrists and aching back, there was the precious secret of my beloved great little book.

Someday—someday!

61

Sweating among the weeds and potato vines ended when the wheat harvest began. Then anyone able to work could find a job, which was easier than to keep it. For it was grueling business wrestling bundles in the burning yellow dazzle of the stubble, under the incandescent sun through the year's longest, seeming-to-be-everlasting days.

But John and I were taking punishment together, and also we were accumulating a working fund for a great venture that we had in mind and heart. We talked about it eagerly after work, lying on our haystack bed under the stars. It was nothing less than to make a grand tour into the free outside world, where a man could be a man and get somewhere. We would spend the remainder of the summer, and maybe the fall, in spying out the land, one might say. Then, if I could get a school, I would teach that winter while John worked in a grocery store; and in the spring, when we were eighteen and unquestionably grown up, we would take off for good.

First of all, I must make certain of a school to teach, if possible. So when it seemed that our working capital was adequate—considering, of course, the superior opportunities in the land of promise—I called on Miss Charlotte White, our county superintendent of schools.

62

I like to think of Charlotte White, a snowy-haired maiden lady whose advanced age remained a guarded open secret. Those who knew her well agreed in private that, whatever her winter count might reveal, "Aunt Lottie" had not been any younger for a long, long while. But it did seem that she had somehow managed to make a deal with time, and she had been returned so often to her high office that "Miss White" had come to signify one of the indestructible realities—a living, self-renewing institution.

Her spare angularity of frame, together with a rock-faced masculinity of mien, might have proclaimed too stern a soul within. But when she smiled, the unforgetting girlhood in her eyes softened the glowing face and made one feel that, despite her old hostility to sin, she would be kind even to Satan himself—but, mind you, *firm!* For just beneath the deceiving surface there was a rich deposit of that precious human stuff of which the blessed aunties of the race are made forever.

I presented my case to the august lady with misgivings, but she soon reassured me. Yes, there was a vacancy in District 55, some twenty miles west of town, beginning the first Monday in December. There were several big boys in the neighborhood, and school must wait until cornhusking was well over. She would recommend me; but perhaps it would be well for us to have a better understanding of each other.

Whereat she began a friendly little talk about religion in

general. It wasn't Sunday-like or churchy, and she didn't rub it in. But for the first time I recalled my *Tentiad* with more regret than glee. She must have known all about my "epic" escapade, but not a word was spoken about it. When she had finished, her face went luminously gentle as she peered into my eyes. "And don't forget to pray, John," she said. "Don't forget to pray."

I went forth with a light heart.

63

Several days later, with a horse and buggy borrowed from my Uncle George, I drove to District 55 and called on Moderator Jensen. He was a well-fed, outsize man, and when I announced my desire to teach his school, I thought I caught the flicker of a quizzical grin about his stubbled mouth as he fixed me far below there with a cocked, appraising eye.

Evidently my credentials were sufficiently impressive. They included a second-class certificate with first-grade markings and a brief letter from Miss White. After spelling out the letter painstakingly, he allowed that I must be plenty smart enough, but what about "them ornery boys?" Last year, it seemed, they had playfully put the teacher out the window, and she never came back. What "them boys" needed was somebody to "thrash hell out of 'em," and it was clear that he thought I didn't look the part. But I boldly insisted that I knew I'd like the boys, and we'd be friends before a month was out. It was rather like whistling in a graveyard, but it worked.

W—e—l—l—seeing nobody else—had applied—he guessed they'd try me out.

Thirty dollars a month for four months. The district would furnish corncobs for fuel, and I'd do the janitor work myself.

He signed the contract with an air that seemed to mean, "And don't forget you asked for this!"

64

Having procured a school to teach and completed preparations for the Grand Venture, John and I thought it proper to have a bit of recreation before leaving home.

Wisner, the center of a German community some twenty miles south of us, was about to have a rip-roaring Fourth of July celebration, according to posters scattered liberally about the country. And there we went with our borrowed horse and buggy.

It was a considerable distance from anywhere to yonder in those leisurely days when most roads were still in their rutted infancy and horsepower was still a function of horses. Also, the way would steadily lengthen with the ascension of the midsummer sun. Considering our walk-awhile, jog-awhile progress and the need for frequent pauses, with an occasional friendly drink at a roadside windmill, we'd need plenty of time for the journey. So we were up and rolling in the still, cool white of daybreak.

When we arrived, the hitching racks had begun to fill up, except along two principal business blocks of Main Street, reserved for festivities and featured events. Wagons were being parked in vacant lots and on side streets with unharnessed teams tied to the wheels and the wagon beds packed with hay.

As it seems now, there was a bodeful spell of expectancy over the town, as though it were getting set for some big effort. Our country was head over heels in the war with Spain —our first war since Appomattox. The Fourth fell on a Monday, and all day Sunday there had been rumors about a great battle then thought to be in progress between the American and Spanish fleets off Santiago Bay. Everything was said and denied. The gathering of news at the source was difficult and slow, and there was no radio as yet. What reports leaked through the telegraph instruments were garbled and fragmentary. For a time it was believed that our fleet had been destroyed and Admiral Cervera's invincible armada was steaming toward our defenseless Atlantic seaboard cities. But Santiago Bay was far away, the rumors were contradictory; so the celebration would go on as planned.

The half dozen or more saloons, faithful indicators of the social weather, were serving the casual drift of customers. Occasionally a roistering group, making the suds circuit of the village, might noisily breast a bar, demanding a round of foaming tankards for all and sundry. But as yet no soulful tenor had recalled "darling Clementine," and no inspired statesman had viewed the world situation with oratorical alarm. The veteran stein brigades had not yet come into action; and the celebration was still an orgy of lemonade and innocence, with wholesome fun for all the family.

To fill the time of waiting for the picnic dinner and the great speech of the day, some of the lesser attractions, as advertised, were being put on; the foot race of grandmothers, for instance. Old Grandma Copple won it in a breeze, of course. Copples had a habit of winning their foot races. It was in the blood. And, indeed, one of them was the fastest 220-yard man in the world. Now and then the brass band struck up encouragingly, and when it ceased with a brazen clash, the milling populace cheered raggedly. Then once again the chatter and bang of the importunate firecrackers took over in the growing swelter.

The prodigiously strong man, all bulge and brag, had offered his cool one hundred dollars ("Walk right up, folks, and count it yourselves") to any man who could stay a short three minutes in the wrestling ring with him. There were no takers, although the popular demand for the local Samson (an elephantine bartender with a falsetto voice) was clamorous and persistent.

"Take the piker, Lester!"

"Aw, come on, Lester! We're all backing you!"

"Show him up, Lester, the big slob!"

The potato race and sack derby had been run. The greased pig had finally been caught with much rough tumbling and shrill hilarity. Now the people began to drift toward the city park and trickle into the shady grove where the free picnic dinner was about to be served. Two fat steers had been barbecued over glowing logs in a pit, and there were roasted piglets for a side dish, together with all the extras and trimmings furnished by the ladies of the town.

A dripping ice wagon with a cargo of block ice and pony kegs pulled up into the shade of a spreading maple and prepared to fill tin pails at a dime apiece, pail size optional. This convivial activity was once known as "rushing the growler," and was in special favor for family groups and friendly circles.

There was a notable increase in the service after the arrival of the wagon. Meat carvers, bread slicers, sandwich makers sweated and toiled manfully, keeping the tray-bearing waiters supplied with heaped-up food for the hungry multitudes.

The hen-coop medley of tangled voices, peculiar to the feeding of any human assemblage, slowly softened into a low murmur of gastric satisfaction.

And at last it was time for the speech of the day. Firecrackers impudently loudened in the hush that fell upon the crowd as the Reverend Hiram Saunders, minister of the First Baptist Church and speaker of the day, mounted the plank platform in company with the Mayor and other local dignitaries.

No doubt the Reverend Saunders had been chosen partly for his reputation as an eloquent orator, but more for his moral and spiritual stature. Notably pious, full of good works, and a faithful servant of the Lord, his words and presence, it was thought, would tend to raise the patriotic festival to a loftier level than it had ordinarily reached in the recent past.

After a powerful invocation, which gave Providence a thorough briefing on human needs and frailties, the reverend launched forth into his oration. He began with a review of our involvement with Spain, reaching a dramatic climax in the blowing up of our battleship, the *Maine,* in Havana Harbor on February fifth. Thereafter he developed his theme with mounting eloquence and dramatic power until he was dealing with nothing less than the immemorial duel between Jehovah and Satan, the endless struggle between Good and Evil (we being definitely on the side of the angels).

Finally it began to become evident that he was approaching his peroration; and indeed it was not too soon, for his voice had begun to hoarsen and crack from the outdoor straining to be heard and he was sweating profusely.

We friends and fellow Americans, he observed, were assembled there at a solemn moment in the long lists of time. A great principle was at stake. We were being weighed in the balance, and must not be found wanting. Surely it was the hour for serious soul searchings and, verily, if we proved worthy, the God of Battles would be with us; and who then could prevail against us? Our noble boys had already flocked to the dear old flag, joining the great crusade to fight and, if need be, to die for all of high and holy.

The reverend had reached a stage of calisthenic fury. Waving his arms aloft, he shouted, "We shall triumph, for our cause, it is just. We will sweep the perfidious Spaniards out of the Western Hemisphere! We will drive the dastards into the sea!"

A sudden hush of astonishment closed over the hoarse cry. *Wh−a−t?*

Did he really say it—the old fighting word we commonly spelled with a *b*? It was unthinkable but it was unmistakable!

Had one been observing the crowd from aloft, no doubt he would have noted the ripple of a shock wave spreading over the audience with the progressive realization.

Some wag, no doubt delighted to know the reverend was a regular fellow like himself, let off a roaring guffaw, leaped to his feet, and cheered wildly. Whereat the whole audience arose with laughter and cheers that went on and on. At length the brass band got into the act with the "Stars and Stripes Forever" played in a frantic tempo.

During the pandemonium the good man stood perplexed and lonely in the speaker's place, evidently wondering *what in the world — and was he really as good as all that?*

65

It was midafternoon now. The dust and shouting of the pony races along Main Street had subsided. The idle crowd jostled aimlessly about, having a problematical good time just being together there in the stifling slant of the sun. Now and then the *wham* of a maul came from a striking machine where the brawny exhibited their prowess to a bevy of bystanders, mostly admiring little boys.

A spell of peace and good will had descended upon the people, still pleasantly aware of a plentiful dinner with liquid refreshment. The Ferris wheel was doing a moderate business; and the merry-go-round, close-herding its galloping horses, droned its sole tune with hypnotic monotony. Even the concessionaires cried less stridently from their booths.

The spirit of *Gemütlichkeit* was abroad among the people. In the bars a stranger was no longer strange. There a snatch of familiar song made kin of those who heard; and hairy-chested men, blowing off the foam together, embraced like long-lost brothers.

Verily, we were having a right nice quiet time that afternoon, despite the drowsing heat; and we were looking forward to the big display of fireworks that would begin in the cooling of the dusk.

Then it began to happen!

The hurdy-gurdy blare of the merry-go-round died out. The Ferris wheel slowed down to a full stop with several passengers still aloft. A full-toned voice crying through a megaphone silenced the hucksters. It was the Mayor of the town who was about to make an important announcement. The word traveled slowly until all faces were turned to where His Honor stood in a wagon bed, the focal center of a spreading hush.

Ladies and gentlemen, fellow Americans!

The telegrapher at the railroad station had just handed him the first pages of an Associated Press news story then still coming over the wire. He would read it to us as it was delivered to him.

Yesterday (Sunday, July third) the American fleet under Admirals Sampson and Schley had won a great victory off Santiago Bay, Cuba. The entire Spanish fleet under Admiral Cervera had been destroyed! The cruisers *Vizcaya* and *Marie Teresa* were beached and still burning! Spanish casualties were extremely heavy, but only one American life had been lost! The war was practically over, and the American flag was flying over the Governor's palace in Santiago!

A roar of wild applause, wave on wave, swept over the crowd, overwhelming the voice of the Mayor. Only those near where he stood could hear what he was reading, but the gist of the continuing story was abroad and spreading.

Then, as someone later remarked, all hell broke loose! The band struck up *A Hot Time in the Old Town Tonight,* playing it over and over, and the whole crowd broke into a windstorm of song.

Truly there was going to be a hot time. It had already begun, for now kegs were being rolled out into the middle of Main Street, there to be set up and tapped for free drinks on the town. And round about them jostling, singing revelers danced gaily in the dust.

I was shouldering and dodging my way through the crowd down Main Street in search of John, whom I had lost somewhere in the excitement, when I found myself jammed into the doorway of a saloon by the surging, singing crowd. As there seemed to be no escaping suffocation either inwards or outwards, I managed to emerge upwards, like a cork in a flood. There were two spacious bay windows protruding into the street, and within one of these stood a billiard table which I mounted, seizing a billiard cue by the way as a sort of accident insurance; for it was plain that a momentous debate was getting under way just below me in the boiling press of men. It seemed to be concerned with the relative merits of the Mauser rifle, used by the Spaniards, and the Krag-Jörgensen, used by the Americans. According to a beefy

German bartender, the Mauser was infinitely the better rifle, if not even more so. And look who invented it. The Germans, of course! As for that clumsy fence post, the Krag, you couldn't hit a flock of tame red barns with it once out of three at a hundred yards. Even the divinely condemned Irish could have invented a better blunderbuss!

Alas! That was no way at all, at all, to address Jimmy Conley, defender of Krags and all things anti-German, for Jimmy was Irish and belligerently proud of the fact. Of middle height, slender and lean, he hardly looked the hero of his storied brawls among his natural enemies, the "Dutch."

While I prefer not to repeat Jimmy's rejoinder, I may say that it seems to have been overharsh and repugnant to family pride. At any rate, the bartender complained loudly to the world at large that no man could speak that way about his dear old mother.

Jimmy was bellied up to the bar with a foot on the rail at the moment of crisis, and the full mug of freshly drawn beer struck him squarely in the face.

That was it!

A sudden lull fell upon the uproar as Jimmy stepped back, a white glare in his eyes and bloody beer foam on his grinning face. With a catlike spring he vaulted the bar, landing a fist on a chin as he came over the top. The man with the sainted mother and the unfortunate chin disappeared beneath a tangle of Jimmys and the next of three barmen on duty. The third escaped through the door at the end of the bar, and after him raged the defender of Irish honor.

When Jimmy emerged into the agitated crowd of the bar-room, the air seemed to fill with flying fists. By now he was "fighting at both ends and in the middle," as they used to say of him in those heroic days; for what he did not do with fists and heels, he did with his butting in the belly of his foe.

It was good indeed that I had seized my vantage point upon the billiard table. I had a reserved front seat, one might say, and I could look down into the melee with a minimum of risk. As for the danger of maybe drowning in that whirlpool of

127

angry men, I backed against the wall, gripped my reassuring cue, and hoped for the best.

Of course nobody noticed me. Jimmy was fighting his way toward the front door, a ring of cautious assailants moving with him in its center like a pack of rabbit dogs about a wildcat.

When Jimmy reached the front door, the outside crowd gave way a bit before that face; and Jimmy, cupping hands about a bleeding mouth, gave forth with Irish yells that brought replying yells from here and there across the milling crowd.

Word had already spread abroad that the Dutch were ganging Jimmy Conley; and the blood cry for help had reached the Layhes and the Neary boys, as usual on the prowl for trouble and perhaps a merry fight.

The sides of my bay window gave me a clear view up and down Main Street, and I could follow the gathering of the clan by the agitation of the people where sporadic fights broke out. I fancy it would be something like witnessing the invasion of a virulent skin disease enormously magnified. I could actually see the fight infection spreading from man to man, as from cell to cell. Relatively healthy areas of the social body would suddenly flare up and swell, erupting into angry fever spots of writhing bodies. Maybe someone would hit someone on the back of the head in front of him for the cogent reason that someone had hit him on the back of his head for no reason at all. Anonymous retaliation would fall upon anonymous retaliators. Maybe a fistful of knuckles would land midmost the nearest facial features in the melee of yelling faces. Whereupon, perhaps, some bewildered innocent went under with a gratuitous wallop on the jaw. And did anyone pause to question what seemed to be the trouble, and why did someone hit him, quite likely he took his answer on the nose.

"If you see a head, for the love of God, hit it!" That, they say, made a Donnybrook Fair; and that is what I was seeing in the crowd-packed block of shouting men and screaming women.

128

Meanwhile, battered Jimmy, backed up against a wall, had been taking on all cautious comers as they came, biding the arrival of relief. And now a cry went up over the crowd: "The Layhes are coming! The Neary boys are coming!"

And indeed they were!

They were coming in close formation from up the street, raising the Irish yell as they came. From my window I could follow their charge by the boiling wake of tumbled, scrambling men they left behind them.

The battle did not last long after that. The unorganized opposition melted away rapidly and the fighting just petered out in the general exhaustion. They hoisted Jimmy to their shoulders for a ride of triumph, and there was desultory cheering.

Then the sun went down upon the stricken field. In the cooling of the twilight, all along the grassy parkway by the street, doctors treated the bruises of inglorious heroes; and there was reminiscent laughter over details of the fracas.

Then, while the soft summer sky blossomed with fireworks, the band played "The Star Spangled Banner" and we all stood with our hats off. After that we had "Clementine," played ever so softly, and many of us sang it together with gentle laughter.

Finally they played "The Wearing of the Green" just by way of saying "No hard feelings."

66

Immediately after the Battle of Wisner, John and I headed for Kansas City; and now, at last, we were there, with some assorted hopes, four dollars, and a few cents. All the remainder of our capital had gone for a suitcase, some clothing, a pair of railway tickets, and advance rent for a crummy room on lower Main Street.

Everybody seemed to be looking for money, but apparently there wasn't enough of it to go around. Little knots of men idled on street corners, waiting for nothing in particular, or thirsted vainly in front of inhospitable saloons.

An employment agency near the Ninth Street Junction displayed exciting bulletins about good jobs to be had at a dollar a day, but they all seemed to be a long way off. Dull-eyed, lean-looking men read them slowly over and over, finally slouching away down the street in search of a better corner for loafing.

One of my most compelling reasons for going to Kansas City was that I hoped to find a publisher for *The Divine Enchantment*. I had heard of the Hudson Publishing Company, and it seemed reasonable to me that they might be interested. I had carefully typed the manuscript, binding it in an ornamental cover designed to catch the prospective reader's eye. This we had brought with us—our most precious possession. So great was the hope it inspired that for a week or more after arriving in the city we hesitated to put our fortune to the test.

Tomorrow I would confront the Hudson magnates. But when tomorrow came—what if they just said no? After that there would be nothing to hope for. So perhaps it would seem best to wait until the next tomorrow. Then, positively, I would screw up my courage to the limit, take a deep breath, and storm that fearsome citadel of fate. During the period of anxious hesitation, we strolled nonchalantly past the Hudson place of business several times, by way of getting more accustomed to its forbidding aspect.

Finally I decided to plunge and get it over, one way or another. John was most encouraging. What was I afraid of? It was a great book, wasn't it? How did I know they would not just grab it? And if they didn't, it was a big world, wasn't it? And somewhere somebody would be sure to want it, sooner or later.

That morning I put on our best pair of pants, a spare pair that we had bought at a bargain just before leaving home, while we were still in the money. Being nearly new, they would make a good impression.

Leaving John sitting on the curb a short way up the street, I entered the great front door of my first publisher, feigning a brisk manner that I was far from feeling. Happily, a line from my wise old friend, Vergil, occurred to me: "One day we shall rejoice to remember this." It gave me some much-needed strength. Maybe when I had written many books, I would be telling this story and having a good laugh over it!

There was a baldheaded man wearing a green eyeshade. He was sitting at a desk, so intent upon what he was reading that he didn't notice me for some time. At length, pushing the eyeshade back upon his forehead, he turned to me with a still-unseeing stare that changed suddenly to a look of questioning surprise.

"Well—?" he said.

The next few minutes required almost more courage than I could summon; but I managed to speak. You see, I had written a book and I thought his firm might want to consider publishing it. I had the manuscript with me. Maybe he would care to look at it.

"What's it all about?" he asked, peering over the top of his glasses at me.

Well, I replied, it was what you might call a mystical poem—about Hindu religion and Vedanta philosophy, you know.

"Oh—o—o—o!" he remarked with a sharply rising inflection. Reaching wearily for the manuscript, he began flipping the pages slowly with an air of cautiously smelling his way along. Finally he shook his head slowly as though perplexed.

"No—o—o—o." They only printed pamphlets, catalogs, telephone directories and such things. Sorry.

He pulled the green shade down over his eyes and resumed his task.

When I joined John sitting on his curb, it was not necessary to tell what had happened.

We did not speak for some time.

67

Our financial condition had worsened rapidly, and now the eating problem had become critical. We had been doing very well indeed with ten-cent meals, which were certainly not to be scorned. A really hungry man, not too fastidious, could dine sumptuously on a dime in those fabulous days when a dollar was still a dollar (if you could manage to get one!). There would be a plate heaped with fried liver and onions, a liberal dish of German fried potatoes, and an unspecified helping or two of baked pork and beans. The pitcher of sorghum was freely usable for dessert. Coffee was optional, and several refills were permitted to sufficiently cheeky customers.

Truly a hungry man could buy a banquet, relatively speaking, with a thin dime. But did you have the dime? That was the embarrassing question. Our supply of dimes was running out, with no source of replenishment in sight. We still had one of our original dollars, but we were hoarding that against some unforeseen emergency. In any case the dollar would be needed for the labor-agency fee, if jobs should be found for us. We had imprudently invested in streetcar rides at a nickel a ride while visiting places where my boyhood had been spent. This had been a serious drain on our resources.

During the forenoons John and I prowled separately about the town looking for an opening. At noon we met to report our luck and to devour a five-cent loaf of bread as a midday filler. We were highly elated when John actually turned up with a job of dishwashing in a restaurant on Twelfth Street for a dollar a day and board. And there was no labor-agency fee to pay!

John went to work the next morning at six and we did not meet again until late that night. He reported a rather grueling experience, working at high speed over a tub of near-boiling water, with the second cook and the waitress bawling for "more plates, more cups, more silver." But it *was* a job. Also it gave plenty to eat; and a dollar was a lot of money (if you didn't have one!).

During the afternoon of the second day after John's employment, I strolled over to Twelfth Street just to see where he was working. And, behold—what did I see in the window? A painted signboard reading "Dishwasher Wanted"!

Hurrah! What a stroke of luck! No doubt *two* dishwashers were needed. John and I could work together. With a high heart I entered and applied for the job at the cashier's desk. Acceptance was almost instantaneous. Thereupon I was ushered into the presence of an awesome personage with the title of second cook. He received me haughtily, proceeding to brief me at length on the nature of my duties. I was told also that I was being taken on trial, and no fooling. Any soldiering on the job, and out I'd go! Then he set me to work with a bucket and mop, wiping up the kitchen floor.

All this while no John was in sight, nor did he show up for work on the supper dishes, which I had all to myself.

Somehow I managed to get through that day, and when I reached our room, with a slab of meat in my pants pocket for John, he was waiting for me with that reassuring grin of his. He had been "let go" without pay because, it was explained, he had eaten more than he had earned.

Apparently I had taken my pal's job away from him. But I didn't go back; and it comforts me still to think of that second cook washing all those dishes by himself until the ready-made sign worked again.

I remember it was several days after the dishwashing fiasco that we stood over a garbage barrel in the alley behind a swank restaurant and considered diving therein for a succulent slice of roast beef. Pride decided it would be better to go hungry. So we did.

68

Clearly, our situation now called for drastic action, and we decided to sell our best pair of pants for whatever we could get. The clothing merchant (and moneylender) down on Fifth Street near Market Square was suspicious and sharply critical of our "merchandise." He would give half a dollar — not a nickel more. It was too much. Maybe we stole them pants anyway — how should he know? The cops might come along and make him give them up. Also, he added with a sneer, look at the way them pants was soiled in the seat! *A — sha — a — amed* we should be!

John was freely speaking his mind and offering to fight in defense of our wounded pride when a policeman, strolling by on his beat, stepped into the argument, strongly advising a quieter discussion with somewhat milder language. Also he suggested that he might "run us in" if we didn't get off his beat and stay off.

When the Law had vanished up the street, we were able to compromise with the merchant on the sum of seventy-five cents. It was too much, he protested. There was no percentage in it, but he felt sorry for us boys and wanted to help us.

The fact that we were in funds again renewed our hope, and once more we visited the labor agency with its exciting bulletins about inaccessible jobs. This time, apparently, luck was with us! There *were* jobs for us in the timber up near Sumner. We would be sawing and splitting bolts of hickory wood to be fashioned into axe handles, and we would be paid by the cord. More cords, more pay. It was as simple as that, and entirely up to us.

There *was* one hitch in the deal, however. We would have to find our transportation ourselves; but the agent had our problem partially solved for us already. We would ride a freight train up to Brunswick and walk from there up the branch line to Sumner, where we would report for duty at the local barbershop.

That afternoon, about five thirty, a freight train with oil tank cars would be switching in the railroad yards near the Union Station, which was then in the bottoms at the foot of the Ninth Street Incline. We would climb aboard one of these cars, snuggle up close to the tank, and let the locomotive do the rest. Quite likely nobody would notice us, or care if they did. It was the era of migrant hobos constantly seeking the Big Rock Candy Mountain; and almost every freight train carried its quota of them, just going from where they were to anyplace else. It sounded like an exciting adventure, together with a golden opportunity to make some real money. Camping and working in the timber along a river would be fun after our unhappy city experiences.

The agent's fee was a dollar for each of us; but we settled for our hoarded original dollar and a promise to send another on our first payday. Then, thrilled by our prospects, joyously carefree again, and wolfishly hungry, we ate!

There was only one freight train hauling tank cars to be seen in the yards, and we had no difficulty in boarding it according to instructions. For what seemed to be hours we lay spreading ourselves thin along the rim of the flatcar with the curve of the tank above us. At any moment someone might come and throw us off before the switching was finished and the train could get under way.

After numerous bumping starts and stops chattering up and down the line of cars, the engine away up yonder let off a long, tragic wail, querulously repeated. And we were off at last!

When we had left the yards and the suburbs behind, we sat on the edge of the car with legs dangling over, watching the earth hurrying by a few feet below us, and the distant landscape drifting leisurely into the past.

A gang of boys swimming in a creek that we rumbled across climbed out of the water, waving wildly. No doubt they were envying us our grand adventure.

A curious cow, studying us across the fence, bolted as we whistled for a crossing and fled high-tailed at a panic gallop.

We had eaten our fill; our hopes were high; we still had a little money; and we were making a story that would be good to tell.

Clickety-click, clickety-click — who-who — whoooo!

The twilight came early with a towering cloud black against the sunset; and as we bored into the night, it began to rain, soon increasing to a downpour. By lightning flares I could see John huddled yonder with back to the tank, water running off the point of his nose over that grin of his. I crawled over close to him, and for a while we shouted in each other's ears. We couldn't talk for the hollow droning of the rain on the evidently empty tank, the crack and roll of thunder, and the overall deep rumble of the train. There was nothing to do but sit and take the chill flood miserably. Sometime the rain would quit. Sometime it would be day and the sun would shine again. Sometime the train would stop.

It did stop, at long last, in a little town whose main street, now asleep in the drowsy light of idle storefronts, faced the railroad tracks. There we pulled into a siding to await the passing of a passenger train from the east. By now the storm had ceased, but a steady rain was falling. While we were waiting there, brazenly visible, a brakeman in a raincoat came along, swinging a lantern, and brusquely ordered us off the train.

After I had insisted upon giving him the story of our one chance to work at Sumner and our great need of a job, he asked if we had any money. I told him we had a quarter between us, which was true; and he agreed to let us ride to Brunswick for that. He wouldn't take it, we were assured, if he thought it was all we had. I gave him our last money, and when the passenger train had roared by, our freight backed out onto the main line, and we were off again into the inky drench of the night.

The rain finally tapered off into a light drizzle; and, being thus relieved, the need for sleep became a burden on us. By the lessening flares of the retreating storm I could see John slumped over in a sprawling huddle, sound asleep. It would not do for both of us to sleep at once, so I forced myself to sit stiffly upright, staring into the vaguely flowing world out yonder. I thought thus to control the creep of drowsiness, and for a while it worked.

Then I must have nodded!

When I came suddenly awake in a clutch of terror, I was leaning out over the edge of the flatcar, staring at the earth that flowed beneath me like a dark river. By the flare of distant lightning I could see John still sprawled in abandoned sleep, and the sight helped to quiet my pounding heart.

I nodded no more that night.

69

When our train stopped once more, far out into the dark somewhere, it was raining hard again and there was a heavy wind. Evidently we had run into another thunderstorm. I pressed close to John and we had the comfort of a mouth-to-ear conversation for a while. By flashes we saw there was a station house down yonder in the dark, but we had no notion where we were. Fearing to be discovered and kicked off the train, we hugged the flatcar floor and waited for something to happen.

For a long while nothing at all happened, except lightning, which threatened to betray us, nearly constant thunder, and the lashing rain upon our backs.

By and by a passenger train, with cozy windows winking complacently at us, came screaming hoarsely out of the dark and roared back into the dark.

We had already begun to move when a man with a lantern

loomed up, yelling for us to "get the hell off that car or he'd come and kick us off." We got.

Our train moved off without us, and there we stood, forlorn, half drowned in the pitch-black sop, with no notion as to where we were. Hand in hand, we started walking along the track, with no clear idea as to why we did it except that walking felt better than standing in the dark and rain.

Suddenly by a lightning flash we saw a corncrib quite near the track, and just beyond it loomed the bulk of a house. There would be a roof over that corncrib; so we entered, and the lightning revealed a pile of old rag carpets in a corner. They must have been very dirty and probably rat-infested; but we burrowed under them and, free from the punishing rain and the chill, swooned away into an abysmal sleep.

Almost immediately, it seemed, the storm had ceased, and there was early daylight. Now we noted that we were only a few feet from the back door of a home—probably the section foreman's. Smoke was rising from a kitchen chimney, and we feared there might be a misunderstanding of our character and intentions if we were discovered there. So we fled down the track.

A sign on the station house revealed our whereabouts. We had slept in Brunswick!

70

When the sun came blazing up in a sky washed clear by the storm of the night, we were already afoot on the railroad track to Sumner, eighteen miles away. A lonely old apple tree in a forsaken orchard by the right-of-way gave us a free breakfast, and by noon we were entering the town. Several people whom we met on the street paused to eye us suspiciously; and we must have appeared shocking. But we were triumphant, nonetheless, having arrived; and now to report for duty at the barbershop!

The barber was busy with razor and tongue, recounting some detailed experience to his captive audience while deftly scraping the lathered countenance of his customer. The face emerged finally, but the highly circumstantial tale continued; for there were hot and cold towels to be applied, various ointments to be slapped on and rubbed in. Also there was hair to be combed. (And how about a haircut today? No?)

When finally the patient escaped from his chair and the unfinished story ceased, the barber turned to us with a start of surprise.

"Bath?" he inquired. Well, the water wasn't hot yet. We could come back about three maybe. A bath was a quarter — and use all the water you wanted — soap and towel free.

By the way, where were we from? Live around these parts somewhere?

When I had told him we had just come from Kansas City to work in the hickory timber and were reporting to him for duty according to instructions, he made a long face and regarded us sadly for a while. Then he said, "You boys pretty good swimmers?" Because, he explained, them hickory bottoms was all of four foot under water and gettin' deeper. Worst flood he could recollect, boy and man.

There was only one thing to do, it seemed to us — return to Kansas City and make another trial for a job before giving up. Our grip was there with some clean clothes and our most precious possession — the manuscript of my book, *The Divine Enchantment*. The very thought of the latter now seemed to increase the possibilities of success enormously. Surely we had overlooked some opportunity that would be clear to us now that we had traveled far only to find more trouble.

But we had no money. Perhaps the barber, being implicated in the matter, would help us. But business was "awfully slow here of late." Men seemed to be shaving their own whiskers and having their hair cut by their wives at home. It was tough going, and he had to think of the kids. But when I brought forth my razor, our one symbol of respectability, he agreed to loan us fifty cents on it. We could send him the money sometime and he would return the razor by mail.

As for the trip back to the city, a passenger train would stop at Sumner for a minute or two at ten o'clock, and we could try our luck at riding the "blind baggage." This was a false entrance to the front end of a baggage car—a roofed-over platform with steps on each side and a door that did not open. The blind baggage followed the engine tender, and it could not be reached by the crew when the train was under way. Nor was it then vulnerable to attack—except perhaps by some playful fireman, with a wry sense of humor, flipping coal at a dodging traveler.

After devouring a ring of "baloney" and some crackers, we slept on a big log lying beside the road outside of town.

It was getting dark and sprinkling rain when we awoke. Maybe our barber would still be up and around, and we could spend some time with him before our train came by. He was there—and so also was a small convention of towns-men. When we paused before the shop's show window to read the clock on the wall, the talk within suddenly ceased, and all faces were turned toward us with blankly unaccepting stares. So we continued down the street toward the station.

The clock on the barbershop wall had said 9:30, and soon we would be out of this inversely blessed town forever and ever. It was raining steadily now, but we were lying well protected under the extended eaves of the station. According to our calculation, the blind baggage would stop at the end of the station platform near where we were. We would lie in wait there, as little conspicuous as possible, until the train was gaining speed after its brief stop. Then we would rush out and onto the blind to ride safe and dry until the next stop, at least—maybe all the way to Kansas City.

Presently, as we lay there under the eaves listening anxiously for the whistle of our approaching train, three men bulked darkly over us. They carried lanterns and had metal stars on their raincoats. One of them, we soon learned, was none other than the town marshal himself, commonly known to floaters as "the bull." Scorning danger, he had come in line of duty, with two husky deputies, to arrest us for the dangerous vagrants we might be.

While the two others were going over John, the man of law seized me by the collar and, yanking me to my feet, began frisking me for a gun. For a breathless moment he almost found one, too—the big-bowled pipe in my hip pocket!

He'd have to take us in, he said, because being vagrants was "agin the law." When I ventured to protest that we were trying to get out of his town, and would soon be gone if he'd let us alone, he reminded me forcefully that stealing rides on railway trains was also "breakin' the law."

So, herded by three strong men and true, with an occasional poke in the back as a reminder of authority, we marched out into the rain and up along Main Street. Some porches in front of business places were now largely occupied by reserved seats for the curious, and our triumphal progress toward jail was apparently enjoyed by all.

The village bastille was located in a lonely spot just outside the far end of town. It was a cramped cubicle, stoutly built of oak planking against all criminal assault. A pair of stingy, iron-barred windows peered curiously into the free world outside.

When the great key of the law threw back the bolt of the lock and the heavy door whined wide upon its rusty hinges, an odorous blast that might have been the veritable bouquet of crime burst forth gaggingly upon us. Into this dark and fragrant hole they bum-rushed us, leaving no doubt as to who was boss around there. Then, having lighted a coal-oil lamp set in a little cage up on the wall, they went out, slammed the door, and shot the bolt—a fearful sound to recall.

There were bunk beds in a corner. There was a chair. There was a rusty stove.

We sat there staring at each other in the dingy light without a word.

There was the homesick, bustling murmur of rain upon the roof.

Then off yonder in the lonely night there was the long

141

good-by-forever wail of a locomotive on its way to Kansas City.

71

I do not remember lying awake very long that night. I do recall the slamming of the door, the clank of the bolt, the claustrophobic horror of being locked in a dusky hole with the only key in all the world possessed by a hostile stranger.

I remember John's deep breathing in the bunk above me. I remember trying to visualize the marshal reading my *The Divine Enchantment,* but the picture was fuzzy.

Someday—someday—maybe we would rejoice—

Exhaustion is a merciful comforter. All at once the stingy little windows were full of morning! There was another clanking of the bolt. The door whined open, and lo, behold! the marshal, with only one deputy, waving us out into the bright, incredible beauty of the day.

There were no cheery good mornings, no jovial biddings to breakfast, no fondly lingering farewells. We headed at an eager pace for the open road bordering the railway track. We were off on foot for Kansas City, more than a hundred miles away. No more trains for us! No more jails!

When we were a comfortable block away from the law, John had his parting shot. Making a megaphone of his hands, he shouted merrily, "Thanks for the ham and eggs, Marshal!" There was no response.

My God! It was good to be free!

The mounting sun poured blessings upon us, clammy still from our soakings in the rain.

We still had a little money from our razor loan, and a country store halfway to Tina furnished us a banquet lunch.

That day we must have covered better than twenty miles; and after a hearty supper of cheese and crackers, with plenty to drink at a cattle trough, we slept in a haystack near the railroad right-of-way.

72

Our brief Sumner campaign had been a disaster, and our return to Kansas City was no strategic retreat. It was, rather, a wild rout. We followed the railroad track, lived, after a fashion, off the country, and slept whenever it got dark. Our practice in long-distance walking with little to eat served us well, at first. Railroad ties were not spaced to accommodate pedestrians, the required stride being either bounding or mincing; but by the end of the second day we had covered about forty miles on meager cheese-and-cracker lunches. The proceeds of our razor loan were now exhausted, excepting ten cents which we felt obliged to save for crossing the bridge at Kansas City.

Several times during the days of hunger ahead we had another longing look at those nickels, which stood for two big filling loaves of bread. Should we take a chance on the ferryboat at Kansas City? Maybe we could steal a ride. Maybe some farmer, hauling garden stuff to market, would let us ride across with him in his wagon. The gnawing in our bellies argued against our reasoning; but we saved the nickels!

Now and then there would be an orchard or a garden in the bottoms, for the railroad followed the river valley much of the way. The only apples we found were greenish, but they filled; and so did new potatoes, "graveled" in convenient potato patches. Heretofore the idea of begging was repugnant to us, but green apples and raw potatoes changed our minds.

There was a prosperous-looking farm home, and I knocked at the back door. A man appeared, looking much taller than men should be. My pal and I wanted to work for something to eat, I managed to tell him. Did he have anything for us to do? He looked me over with a deprecating grin. "You don't want to work!" he said, and slammed the door. I hope to meet that man in Heaven and have a friendly talk with him.

Once a gray-haired, grandmotherly woman, with a scared look on her otherwise gentle face, gave us each a piece of bread and butter. But she regarded us cautiously through a half-closed door; and it was clear that we were not of her species.

Nights on the river bottom were shivery cold, and we tried burying our bodies in sand. But swarms of mosquitoes fed on our faces; and after a while the sand was as chilly as we. Once we climbed a bluff to sleep; but late in the night we awoke with chattering teeth in a dripping fog. So we climbed back down to the railroad, walked the track until morning, and slept in the sunlight much of the day.

The only cheering human encounter on the whole journey was with a pair of professional hobos. We met them on a sunny afternoon, strolling toward us in leisurely fashion. Raggedly clothed in misfit hand-me-downs, with stubbled faces and straggling hair, they might have hired out as scarecrows.

"What's the hurry, boys?" asked one of them. "Because, if you're fixin' to catch something, you ain't going to. We been there and back. It ain't there."

We sat down together on the grassy embankment for a spell of rest and a visit.

"You boys look hungry," said the more affable one. "Got any grub?"

We hadn't. Couldn't find any work to do.

"Work!" he sniffed. "That makes a man humpbacked!"

He rummaged in a bag he had been carrying at the end of a shouldered stick, and came up with two sandwiches.

"Working back doors," he explained. "It's good business if you know how."

We were nice-looking boys, he observed. Maybe a little dirty; but that was only natural, and it would rub off. The women would feel sorry for us and we ought to do well.

144

But remember not to bother with the big rich houses. Stick to the nice little places that maybe needed a bit of paint and had flowers blooming in the front yard. Them was the best. When we were talking to the lady of the house, we should always take off our hats and say "Ma'am." Sometimes she would feed us out on the back porch because we looked lousy. Then we could manage to say something about our mothers, and, like as not, she would fetch out a piece of pie.

At parting, we were admonished again not to hurry, "because it just ain't there, boys."

And, by the way, if anybody should want to know, we could tell 'em that we saw the Foster boys from the old home place way down in the Bassakreeny Mountains.

One day I noted that John was lagging far behind and limping. When I stopped to wait for him, he approached me with that grin of his and held up one of his feet for my inspection. One side of a shoe sole had been worn away by the sharp-edged ballast on the railway grade, and the naked foot was oozing blood. "Talk about your heroes at Valley Forge!" he said, laughing as though it were a good joke. We bandaged the foot with a piece of shirttail, and John resumed the march, using the other side of his foot.

73

During the forenoon of the sixth day out of Sumner we arrived at the railway bridgehead opposite Kansas City. A mile or more upstream was the wagon bridge for which we had saved our nickels. We were bone-weary from hopping ties for more than a hundred miles with little food and sleep. There straight ahead of us was the empty railroad trestle taking the river at a leap. If we hurried, might we not cross before a train could come? As far as we could see in every direction, all was quiet in the brooding summer day, and no one was in sight.

But what if we *should* be caught by a train out on the bridge?

It was terrifying to think of clinging to a stringer and hanging out over that ropy current a dizzy drop below while waiting for a train to rumble over. But if we made a dash for it and went fast—? We could save those nickels for bread!

Finally John settled the matter. "Come on, kid," he said, "let's go!"

And we went at a brisk trot, timing our shortened strides to the narrow spacing of the bridge stringers. Although falling through between the ties was unlikely, there was a dreadful fascination about the flowing flood beneath, and it was hard to keep one's eyes on the solid footing. Anxious listening for the feared whistle of a locomotive made the way seem endless. And when at last it ended, we began to fear police. If they had seen us, we would probably be jailed.

But luck was with us this time; and having reached the other side, we soon found a place to spend our nickels advantageously. In the slums along the railway there was a little eating place run by the Helping Hand Institute for bums and the disinherited generally. Its specialty was pancakes with sorghum—three of them, very durably made and as large as a dinner plate—no extra charge for molasses. All this was to be had for a nickel, if you had one. If you didn't, there would still be two cakes, undiminished in size and durability, with a limited helping of sorghum. Coffee was on the free list, night and day, no doubt in recognition of the fact that Trouble is timeless and a poor sleeper.

Being relative plutocrats with the qualifying nickels, we were allowed considerable latitude in the matter of sorghum consumption. There was a sizable pitcher full of it on the table, and we floated our cakes in the precious stuff, eating the mixture with spoons. The attendant did seem to view our devastating hunger with some alarm, but charity prevailed, and he made no comment.

74

So we were back in Kansas City, and it seemed our hobo friend was right. By going fast we had overtaken nothing, and by going far we had found nothing.

But we had not yet seen our precious manuscript again. Perhaps that would make all the difference somehow. There was a touch of magic in the thought of it; and often it had made fatigue and hunger seem momentarily like mere details in a holding story we were living and someday would tell.

We found our crummy room on lower Main Street closed to us. Our rent was in arrears almost a week, and we'd have to pay in advance if we came back. I argued with our landlord, and after some hesitation he agreed to let us wash up a bit and change shirts. Thus, I had pointed out, we would be in better shape to get jobs and earn the money we owed him. Having won this much, I made an equally bold plea for possession of the manuscript, maintaining that it could be of no use to anyone but myself and might help me get a job. After examining the curious object for a while, he seemed well convinced that nothing could be lost by letting me have it.

Things were looking up, and I had an idea. When we first arrived in Kansas City, I canvassed the tombstone shops, but no one needed a marble polisher. There was one proprietor, however, who was kinder than the others, and he seemed to take a human interest in me. So I decided to call on him again, taking the manuscript with me. John said he would see what he could do collecting handouts while I was trying my luck among the tombstones.

It was near closing time when I arrived, but the proprietor received me cordially, remembering my former visit. He was sorry that he still had no job for me, but money was tight. People seemed to be dying as much as ever, he observed, but the late-lamented could wait for their memorials, having nothing else to do.

I managed to introduce the manuscript, and for some time

he sat examining it, apparently forgetting my presence. At length he asked if he might take it home and return it in the morning.

Indeed he might!

John turned up that evening with a triumphant grin and several sandwiches.

We spent that night in a charity flophouse down on Fourth Street, the price of admission being nothing at all but need. It was a gloomy, cavernous place, redolent of misery and formaldehyde. Once, according to legend, it had been a variety theater—a temple of ribald mirth; but that was in the good old days before the rat invasion.

There were bunks arranged in tiers about the walls, and a few oil lamps in brackets. All night long a watchman with a swinging lantern made his stealthy rounds; and always when I awakened from a wink of troubled sleep, that ghostly presence was abroad, casting weird shadows of himself about the room.

It would have been an awesome place to waken in the dead of night remembering one's sins. There was more than literary import in my thought of Dante; for surely the place was full of tortured souls in Purgatory, halfway to Hell—and slipping. They moaned and muttered, tossing in uneasy sleep, or sometimes cried aloud in some too vivid dream.

John's bunk and mine were standing foot to foot, so that either of us, rising on an elbow, could see the other. Once I wakened in the eerie half-light of the few oil lamps, thinking I had heard John calling *hist, hist.* And truly he *was* sitting yonder like a newly resurrected ghost, making comic faces at the world! My belly laughter brought the roving watchman with his lantern, to find us sweetly sleeping.

75

Truly there *was* magic in the manuscript!

Next morning I was waiting outside the tombstone shop when the proprietor arrived. He seemed noncommittal and a trifle cool as he handed me the precious package containing our masterpiece. Then, having attended to several minor matters about the shop, he said: "That's your place over there — that slab of marble. We're giving it the final polish. I can't afford this, my boy; but I think we're going to hear from you sometime."

I don't know where that imperishable marble may be, but I think it must be identifiable by its special glow; for I went at it with a singing heart and rubbed with all my might.

During that forenoon, while busy with polishing, my new boss questioned me about our circumstances. As a result he set my pay at fifteen cents an hour and advanced enough to cover our room rent, together with a temporary allowance for food.

John was sent to settle the rental account; so we had a roof over our heads again and clean clothes to wear. As for the food allowance, John insisted on saving it "just in case," undertaking to feed us by "collecting," as he called it.

The shop was built on the street corner into the side of a steep hill sloping eastward to Main. A wooden sidewalk ran diagonally across the open window of the shop; and there John liked to take his seat and watch me, busy at my job below him. I can still see him dangling his legs and making faces at me when the boss wasn't looking; and I can hear him saying in a stage whisper: "Work, you lazy son-of-a-gun, you! It's good for your health."

An hour or so before noon or supper, he would disappear, to turn up again at eating time with his "collections" in a paper sack, along with droll accounts of his kitchen-door encounters with housewives. Owing, perhaps, to that engaging grin of his, he soon became a notably efficient "collector," announcing, on occasion, that he was "the one and only woman around this house, by god"—and I'd better like his cooking!

76

Since our disorderly retreat from Sumner we had gradually come to accept the painful truth that our brave venture into the great wide world was a sorry failure. Obviously the great world didn't want us, and more and more our thoughts turned toward home.

When I had worked out my advanced wages, with several dollars extra, we began hanging around the stockyards in the hope of picking up cattle passes to Omaha. We were in poor condition to bum our way on trains, because of the food we had eaten as well as the lack of it; and there was not enough money in sight for carfares. The passes were issued to shippers and were good only on the cabooses of stock trains hauling the shippers' stock. Although not negotiable, they were often for sale, and we were hopefully in the market. We had mailed our precious manuscript to my Mother, arranged with our landlord to forward our suitcase later when we should be able to send for it, and said good-by to our tombstone friend.

Several days passed with no luck. Then one forenoon a man came rushing by us, waving a couple of passes that he said were good on a train just about to leave the yards for Omaha. He would sell cheaply to anyone ready to go. How much? Three dollars. Too bad! We had only a dollar and a half. "Sold!" he said; and together we hurried out into the yards to find our train. A brakeman, glancing at our passes and at us, grinned and waved us aboard the caboose. Almost immediately the train began to move, and we were off again, busted as usual, but now headed for home and happy.

We were in luxury now, sitting on the hard benches of the caboose and watching the effortless drift of the landscape past the windows.

Late in the afternoon we pulled into Atchison and, after some bumping and the running clatter of switching, we stopped on a siding in the yards. The two brakemen who rode in the caboose had ignored us utterly, spending the time napping with their hats over their eyes. Now they had disappeared, and we were left to wonder if there was something we should be doing; but there was no one in sight to question.

More than an hour must have passed while we sat on the siding. Then one of our brakemen reappeared and spoke for the first time. "You fellows are on the wrong train," he said. "Yours is leaving the yards now. Come, I'll show you." From the rear platform he pointed to a freight train that was just getting under way.

"But," I protested hotly, "that can't be our train! There's not a cattle car in it, and there should be at least our two!"

He poked me in the ribs and chuckled. "Yeah," he said, "—your cattle!" Then, swinging off the back step, he disappeared.

It was getting on toward night, and a drizzling rain had begun. We were in a strange town with no money and no place to go. It was our old familiar pattern working out again.

Out in the midst of the maze of tracks stood the two-story building of many windows where the train dispatcher and yardmaster operated. It was already brilliantly lighted for the growing dusk, and it gave me a big idea. John and I would bring our case before the officials themselves and demand justice!

When we plunged up the stairs and into the little office full of telegraphic chatter, it was plain to see by the astonishment on the Man's face that we had no right there, and might get kicked out for our effrontery. But there is a tone of authority about a brisk attack audaciously delivered, and I plunged head-on into the business at hand. It must have been a torrent of righteous indignation! Briefly, we had been deliberately misinformed by an employee of the railroad; and as a result our two carloads of cattle would arrive in Omaha with no one to look after them!

The Man had been regarding me in open-mouthed surprise; but when I spoke grandly of our cattle, and even vaguely threatened legal action with a hint of influential connections, he threw his head back and exploded in roaring laughter.

"You'll do!" he said, still chuckling. "But maybe you can ride the eleven o'clock passenger that stops here." Then he told us what to do. We should be waiting on the platform under that floodlight yonder when the train stopped, and as soon as the car was opened and the brakeman had placed his stool under the steps, we should rush past him, into the car, and on through to a rear seat. There we should lie down, and when ordered out, we should refuse to move.

"Show them your passes and give them the same line you gave me," he chuckled. "I think it will work."

It did work famously. We were already moving when the conductor appeared with the brakeman, asking to see our tickets. Of course our passes were no good on passenger trains, but— Then I gave him the story, adding: "You two are bigger than we are, and you can throw us off if you want to; but you'll have to do it, because we're not going to move. And if you do, you may get into trouble."

"Aw, lie down and go to sleep," said the conductor.

So we did. And all through the rainy night we slept in the dry on the plush.

—And by and by, it was the sodden gray of morning in Omaha.

77

We were still more than a hundred miles from home, and walking was our only means of transportation. As yet there were no automobiles, no highways, no traveling by thumb.

Our memory of jail was still a horror, although we joked about it; and we feared that bumming rides on trains might put us back of bars again. The best route home seemed by way of the Fremont, Elkhorn and Missouri Valley Railroad to Pilger, and thence northward across country, passing my Uncle's farm seven miles south of Wayne.

Had we allowed ourselves to consider those hundred miles in a block, all at one time, we might have lacked the courage to push on. But in our long-distance test walks we had developed a system whereby we seemed to be merely nibbling distance at the edge, a relatively easy bite at a time, always prevailing in the moment. We thought it not a bad trick, and we used it now.

The railroad skirted the northern suburbs of the city, and we came to a house whose kitchen door opened near the track. Smoke was rising from the rear of the house; and, being desperately hungry, we decided to try our luck at begging there. We received far more than a breakfast from that house—more than a skilletful of fried potatoes with bread and butter. "I have a boy somewhere," the woman remarked, "and I hope somebody's feeding him." That was more than seventy years ago, and I still can see her face.

During the next thirty-one hours we covered seventy-three miles, reaching West Point the second afternoon at three. Lack of sleep was harder to bear than lack of food. Two farmers had, reasonably enough, refused to let us sleep in their barns. Then we had tried sleeping in a field of tall corn. It gave us a pleasant, closed-in sense of security; but a rain came on, and we wakened in the mud to walk the remainder of the night, feeling our way along the track with the aid of occasional lightning.

Several times, in quest of food, we had been rejected with the slamming of doors. Once I inquired sweetly of a startled housewife if she happened to have some spare food she intended to give her dog. If so, would she please let us work for it—work before eating? She gave us two cold biscuits and hastily latched the screen door.

It happened that we reached the station at West Point,

seventy-three miles from Omaha, just as the afternoon passenger from the city pulled up and stopped with its blind baggage only a few feet from where we stood. We had decided to go on to Pilger, where we would be only twenty miles south of home. Here we had our chance, and by now our weariness surpassed our dread of jails. We reached Pilger unmolested and took the wagon road northward, bound for home at last.

How well we knew this road! Several years before, we had plodded down it in the mud of an all-day downpour, on our way to the Elkhorn for a week of camping and fishing. We were reminded of that adventure now, recalling how our packs became lead-heavy with the soaking; how we built a wickiup with willow withes and long slough grass beside a bayou where the frogs sang all night long in massed chorus; and how we fished for savagely hungry bullheads until the broken moon was lost in the eerie river fog. We even laughed a little (being mellowed, doubtless, by the thought of home) about the way we packed our goodly catch that score of miles "to show the folks"—and caused a small olfactory scandal among the neighbors for our pains.

It was late in the golden afternoon when we decided to rest awhile by a newly made haystack sunning in a friendly roadside meadow. I recall the fragrant softness of the sun-cured prairie grass, the grateful luxury of just letting go and sinking deeper, deeper. We must have fallen asleep almost at once. When we awoke, it seemed the sun was setting.

It was morning!

78

We had now definitely left the hobo lanes of travel; and when we stopped at the first farmhouse up the road to ask for work and breakfast, a kindly old German met us at the door, evidently without the suspicion we had come to expect and dread.

Why, yes, he said, having heard our story briefly sketched, he could use help putting up a late crop of hay in his slough. His boy was in the army, and that left him short-handed until he could find a man. Breakfast was nearly ready, and we could wash up there on the back porch, he said, pointing to a bucket of water with a dipper in it, and a tin wash pan on a bench.

I remember especially the pancakes we ate that morning — the tender buttermilk kind we knew at home, with plenty of eggs, and maybe a pinch or two of motherly affection just to make them fluffy.

Before that breakfast was over we were comfortably at home with the lonely old couple, and John and I had hired out for general farm work. But, first of all, we must see our folks and end their worry about us. Pride forbade a brazen public appearance at home while we were still under the shadow of defeat. We must return with money in our pockets and a good story to tell. Accordingly we arranged with our new friend to spend a night at our homes in town, returning the next day ready to begin work.

It was after sunset when we arrived at the outskirts of town and sat down beside the road to wait for darkness.

When we stealthily entered the back door of my home, my Mother and my sister Grace were sitting at the kitchen table writing anxious letters to us far away somewhere in Missouri. Our sudden appearance out of the dark induced a minor panic. We must have seemed a pair of homesick ghosts. "Oh, please don't take on like that," I said, feeling most unghostly. "Just fry us some potatoes!"

Next morning we left town in the dark before dawn, with a much-needed change of clothing and our pride unimpaired.

A few days later I came down with a violent attack of malarial fever, reminiscent of those hungry mosquitoes down on the Missouri bottoms. John and I had been sleeping in the haymow, preferring it to a stuffy room indoors. That night it seemed I was lying naked to an icy winter wind, desperately striving to draw the snow closer about me for warmth. I awoke with chattering teeth in a torturing spasm of shivers. John was trying to hold a horse blanket about me; but it did no good, for the horror of the cold came from within. Then suddenly I was floating in a vague world of suffocating heat, where dreadful, nameless things were just about to happen.

There was a tremendous vine, and it grew and grew. It came from nowhere, and nothing could stop its growing. It had enormous leaves—elephantine! That was it—*elephantine!* The word took on a life of its own and proliferated madly, until it was everywhere—like the monstrous leaves that sweated with a hot dew of horror—sweated and flopped heavily—*flop, flop* on fences and houses and trees—growing and spreading because nothing could stop them—

And then again the terrifying spasms of cold.

John managed to get me home in a borrowed spring wagon, and for weeks thereafter I lived on quinine and anticipation. My first teaching job would begin December first, and there were those notorious big boys to think about. I had not forgotten the curious look on Moderator Jensen's face when he signed my contract, as though he were saying, "Remember, you asked for this."

The frosty nights came, and by November I was beginning to be my old self again. I must be in good condition when I undertook the enlightenment of those overgrown lovers of learning. So every day I walked and ran in the invigorating Indian-summer weather, preparing myself for possible academic adventures.

79

The snow had begun in the night, and it was still falling lazily when I set out that December morning to teach my first country school. It was a mile and a half from my boarding place, the home of the district treasurer, Joe Dobbin, to the one-room frame temple of learning that sat treeless, grassless, and all but paintless by a lonely crossroads.

Of my numerous walking expeditions, I think that one seemed the shortest, for my forebodings warned me that I was most likely heading straight into trouble beyond my ability to manage. I kept seeing that curious grin on Moderator Jensen's face when he signed my contract, and I had not forgotten his remark that what "them boys" needed was "somebody to thrash hell out of 'em!" And the weeping young lady teacher who was put out the window and never came back. Maybe it was all in fun, but according to my limited sense of humor at the time, it wasn't funny at all. And what if the three husky young cornfeds should decide to have some fun with me?

As I strolled doomward in the whispering silence of the falling snow, vaguely wishing some calamitous happening might relieve me of my obligation, I strove for courage by bragging to myself.

What was I afraid of?

Didn't I have a chest expansion of ten inches? Couldn't I tear a pack of playing cards in two with my hands? Didn't I have the high score on the striking machine—1705? And didn't I have a sure-fire trick wrestling hold that always brought them down with a bang?

Yes; but what good was all that if they all came on at once?

The involuntary stream-of-consciousness answer floated through my head—an absurd fantasy of wishful thought: The biggest of the mischievous trinity went down under a short-arm jab to the jaw (my "ton-of-brick" wallop in the words of the fight-promoter, you may recall). The next in bulk took a quick, vicious heel in the belly and was forthwith out of the contest. The last toppled with a crash, helpless against my secret trick throw. And there they all were! But I didn't believe a bit of it.

And what of Miss Charlotte M. White? I had momentarily forgotten her. Maybe, after all, she was right. Maybe I'd better be praying, the way she advised. And then, maybe those boys were only boys like John and me not so long ago. It might be fun to know them.

As for the young lady teacher who left by the window and went home crying, I knew her well. We had been classmates in the Teachers Course the year before — a pretty, sweet-Alice-Ben-Bolt sort of girl. Why, if she had only known, most likely she could have had those rascals eating out of her hand in no time!

I felt much better after I had started a fire in the schoolhouse. There was something reassuring about the oversize cast-iron stove that stood in the center of the otherwise cheerless schoolroom. The big-bellied glutton had an enormous appetite for corncobs; and when it roared and turned red with eupeptic delight, even a blizzard wind might lose its terrors in a dream of summer sun.

It was giving forth a cozy welcome now as the pupils straggled in, most of them walking, some of the younger ones brought by their parents — a motley collection of ages, sizes, and stages of enlightenment.

There was the little Sweigert boy, convoyed importantly by his big sister — stuffily cloaked, stiffly mittened against the weather. He was about to have his first encounter with the ABC's.

Then there were the big boys, soon to be graduated arbitrarily from their too narrow desk seats. It was for them that school was opening so late, since cornhusking must take precedence over mere book learning. Between these two extremes there was a random scattering of grades from kindergarten to high school.

When the last pupil to arrive had stomped off his snow at the door, there were twenty-some youngsters thirsting boisterously for knowledge in that less than commodious schoolroom. To arrange those in some tentative semblance of order was simply a matter of fitting the lean and stout, the long and short to matching desk dimensions. For instance, there was a "little" fat German boy who, by report, had recently counted up to ten. He knew practically nothing, "knew that in Dutch," as I observed at the time, and enjoyed the apparent status of a fourth-grade education, thanks to liberal feeding at home. I remember wondering how many more pancakes might be needed for promotion to the fifth.

The former teacher's sketchily kept records, together with an incomplete collection of report cards, made possible further sorting of pupils according to academic achievement. Readers, spellers, and arithmetic texts had been stacked on teacher's desk, and these were distributed partly in keeping with records and partly by pupils' selection. By way of verifying some of the choices, reading aloud was required.

Here I am reminded of Willie Hansen's test reading in proof of his proficiency. Willie had evidently enjoyed the fine literary flavor of his first reader, especially the classic saga of the marching children—not to mention Rover and his enthusiastic barking, as suggested by the graphic illustration. Fancy Willie declaiming in a slow, deliberately measured monotone:

"Hear the drum! *Rub-a-dub-dub!* Run, Tom! Run, Ann! Run and bark, Rover!

"The children are coming! See their paper hats! The children are—"

Here there is a prolonged hesitation. The word is *marching*, but it is apparently a poser, so Willie very sensibly resorts to careful spelling.

"M—a—r— m—a—r—"

Suddenly he has it!

"*Rub-a-dub-dub!*" he continues in his accustomed drone, but with a lift of triumph in it.

"*No!*" I protested. "*Marching*, Willie!"

"No—marching—Willie—*rub-a-dub-dub*," he continues intoning monotonously.

This brings down the house and is wildly applauded by the big boys with lusty horselaughs and hand clapping accompanied by vigorous stompings. It looks like incipient rebellion.

I feel my hair standing up on the back of my head. Is this

the beginning of what I had feared? It had been clear from our first meeting that the big boys did not intend to play ball with me. My "Good morning" had been ignored with an exchange of impudent grins among them. There were three of them to one of me, and the smallest of them was no smaller than I.

How I wished for John!

With a show of authority that I did not feel, I rapped my desk sharply with a ruler and yelled, "Stop it!" To my surprise, the laughter ceased! Was this the lull before the storm? I actually took note of the long poker lying under the stove.

At this crucial point a freckle-nosed boy of approximately fifth-grade dimensions changed the ominous mood of the room. Wildly waving an arm for attention, he blurted, "Teacher, Teacher, can't we have a snow fight at noon recess?" And obviously we could, by overwhelming vocal assent!

The suggestion was immensely popular. I myself favored it as a timely diversion as well as a good way for the boys to blow off some excess steam.

So, when we had eaten our lunches and put on coats and overshoes, we prepared for civil war. It was readily agreed that Bill Kendrick, being the largest, should organize and command the rebel forces. Quite as readily, Teacher was chosen to conduct the defense. The body of pupils was then divided into two armies by the time-honored method of "choosing up," as in one-o'-cat baseball. Thereupon a truce of one half hour was declared, that each side might stockpile ammunition. The snow was in excellent condition for balling and rolling, and we of the defense made rude breastworks as well as a goodly supply of snowballs.

When the truce had ended, I gave the signal for the battle to begin by cupping my hands about my mouth and making like a bugle sounding the charge. Immediately the air above the contending forces was full of flying snowballs as the rebel line came on with barbaric yells of defiance. Slowly my skirmish line gave way, fighting stubbornly for every foot of consecrated ground. It was a fearful encounter. Panting warriors wrestled panting warriors, striving to give or to avoid ignominious face-washings in the snow.

Just before the battle began, I had called the youngest and smallest of my army about me and explained how I planned to use them as cavalry, to be held in reserve and sent forward at some critical moment of the battle—the way Napoleon used to do. This I now did, for it was only too evident that the disproportionate number of oversize warriors among the rebels was beginning to tell. Soon my line would break and the enemy would surge forward, swarming over our rude defenses. We would all have our faces thoroughly scrubbed with snow unless the headlong assault could be checked. So I directed my battalion of cavalry to deliver a brisk attack on the rebels' left flank, hoping thus to divert the headlong fury of the frontal assault.

The charge was carried through with highly vociferous gallantry, and the advancing rebel line, feeling the shock, faltered. It looked like the moment for snatching victory from threatening defeat. So I immediately ordered a strong detachment of my heaviest troops to sally forth from the defenses and assail the faltering center of the advance, while my valiant cavalry dogged the vulnerable left flank.

But, alas, the treacherous god of battles was no friend of ours that day! Suddenly a full half of the heavy assaulting forces wheeled like a swinging door to face the threatened flank, the remaining half stubbornly holding my advance line in check. Then, I grieve to remember and shudder to relate, blind panic seized upon my hopelessly outclassed light cavalry. Turning their inglorious rumps to the foe, they fled as vociferously as they had charged.

It was no longer battle. It was unorganized slaughter, a wild rout, and many a captured warrior's countenance was shamefully scrubbed with snow that day of desperate deeds and great despairs.

When the debacle began, I had gone forward to my sagging front line of defense, thinking to stiffen morale by my presence. Then suddenly there was no line. There was no cavalry. There was no foe! Or, rather, the foe was everywhere, for I found myself central and alone in a wild confusion of yells, laughter, and showering snowballs—all apparently meant for me!

It was clear enough that the whole school was united in lambasting Teacher. What was I to do? Should I call school and thus end the hopelessly uneven conflict? I had only to rush in to my desk, seize my brass hand bell, and shake it importantly. But would not such an act be regarded as showing the white feather, a sign that Teacher had cold feet and just couldn't take it?

At this juncture I pulled out my big silver watch, the one resembling a certain variety of sweet turnip, it may be recalled—Pile's watch with which I had so long regulated academic activities in the little college on the hill. I must have appeared a fine, heroic figure of a man, standing there magnificently alone in the midst of the battle fury, calmly contemplating the riddle of old time!

So I stood for quite a while; anyway, long enough to register the impression. Then, raising a stentorian voice above the tumult, I sent forth winged words. "It's time for school," I shouted, "but we're having fun and we'll fight some more!" Thereupon I slammed a fistful of snow into the nearest grin and took a facial plastering in return.

I must say that I really wasn't having any fun. It was clear that I had started something I couldn't stop. I had the proverbial wild bull by the tail, and couldn't even let go. I couldn't win and I couldn't run. How would it all end? Worst of all, what of my dignity as Teacher? Even the kindergarten kids—impudent little rascals—could sneak up and swat me with impunity.

Then suddenly—

Bill Kendrick loomed up before me out of the melee. I can see him yet as I saw him then in a vivid, timeless moment—a robust youth, perhaps a trifle overgrown for his years but amply shouldered and chested like a buffalo bull calf. I caught

162

the triumphant grin upon his flushed face as he stooped in front of me, reaching with his right hand for a fistful of snow. I *saw* and *knew* and I didn't wait for further information!

In that split second Bill had accidentally placed himself in the best possible position for my trick throw. I had only to grasp his right wrist with my left hand, drawing his right arm over my head and around the back of my neck down to my breast, while at the same time curving my right elbow around his right knee from behind. Then I would stand up, and my right hand would grasp his right wrist on my chest. All this would be done with great speed, and Bill would find himself locked on my back with his left leg dangling useless, and he would be unable to strike, bite, kick, or escape. From this position it was a simple matter to dump the struggling burden over my head, back first.

It worked. Bill's size and weight were greatly in my favor now. He came down like a wagonload of brick; and it *was* fun to hear him grunt under the impact of my right shoulder landing in the midst of him!

When I leaped to my feet, I became aware that the tumult was dying out over the battlefield. A ring of spectators was forming about us, and others were running up to see Bill and Teacher in a fracas, as they supposed. But what they saw was a crestfallen Bill shaking the snow off his back and grinning sheepishly about him.

"Sorry, Bill," I said. "That's a mean throw—hard to control."

Then Bill did something that made all the difference. *He slapped his hand on my shoulder and laughed!*

80

The successful encounter with Bill, easily foremost among the big boys and hero of the youngsters, greatly increased

Teacher's prestige and also created a lively interest in the art of wrestling. Occasionally during recess periods when the weather was bad, we would arrange the desk seats in a circle and put on wrestling bouts in the enclosed space. After throwing each of the bigger boys a time or two, Teacher was tacitly regarded as out of the running. It was no longer necessary either to assert or defend authority, and I could use all my energy for teaching. News of my athletic pedagogy got around, and "The Little Teacher," otherwise generally anonymous, came to enjoy a modest measure of fame throughout the school district and thereabouts.

Sometimes when the weather was fine and the prairie was clear of snow, the boys and I would spend a Saturday riding after jack rabbits. Mounted bareback on the best horses of the neighborhood, we would take off, in extended order, across the largely unfenced range land with a greyhound working back and forth in advance, nosily investigating possible hiding places for rabbits. It had been some winters since "old Cyclone," as we called the hound, was a pup, but he was still a lot of dog, with the old sporting heart, and very much one of the boys. Apparently well aware that we could never overtake a jack rabbit with horses, he seemed to know how to prolong the joy of pursuit by cutting across bends in the course, thus keeping the bounding quarry in sight.

It was a wild, heady sport, and not particularly safe, considering the many gopher holes in the ditches we jumped on the run. But it served to develop a happy spirit of comradeship that had a good effect on the school's morale in general.

Truly I "rejoice to remember" these episodes; but I think the richest memories of that winter are concerned with my walks home on Friday nights. It was twenty miles from my boarding place to Wayne—a brisk five-hour jaunt afoot if the roads were clear or a moderate snowfall had frozen firm. I liked best the still, sub-zero nights, when it seemed the very winds had grown too stiff to blow.

It was on such a night that I first undertook the adventure; and this is how it was: Our itinerant preacher, who held services in rotation at various schoolhouses of the region, had reached our place on his visiting circuit, causing panic cackling in our henhouse. (In this connection my Uncle George used to insist that any wise old hen could detect an approaching minister of the gospel by the vibrations from his inordinate appetite for fried chicken; but I don't believe it.) We sat late at table that evening while the jovial reverend dispensed his fund of pulpit anecdotes in a spirit of good fellowship, "as common as an old shoe" despite his profound Biblical learning.

When at last the apple pie and whipped cream had appeared and gone the way of the chicken, it became evident that Brother Wilkins would quickly accept the expected invitation to spend the night with us. Since the only available sleeping space was in the other half of my double bed, the inference was inescapable; and I experienced an unreasonable repugnance for the idea of cuddling up to a preacher between cold sheets. I don't know just why, but it was somehow a matter of modesty. It seemed almost a desecration to share a bed with such a holy man.

Accordingly I shocked the family by announcing my decision to walk home that night, having just thought of an important matter needing attention. Whereupon, with some extra clothing, a woolen muffler, and a heavy walking stick, I set forth into the vast starry hollow of the night while the others were going to bed.

Once the hot blood was set tingling in ears, nose, and cheeks, and the lungs were drinking deep of the exhilarating air, there came an exalting sense of ultimate release from worldly trifles. The sparsely settled country lay sleeping in the trancelike stillness of the cold, and nothing but a panting walker moved in all that awesome hush of things. The rhythmic crunch and whine of footsteps on crusted snow seemed loud. And when I labored to the summit of a high, steep ridge, pausing awhile for breath, tremendous silence, like a flood, came crowding in to listen — listen — listen. Surely some son of Homer knew just such a place and time three thousand years before, when "out of heaven broke the infinite air and all stars were seen and the shepherd's heart was glad."

I could not have lingered long in the searching cold of that summit; but for some spacious lapse of time I must have been as though immortal — divinely alone in a star-haunted cosmos, alone, but, for the wonder of it all, not lonely.

For a long while I had seldom thought of *The Divine Enchantment,* and then only in passing. My living world had narrowed for a season to a schoolroom. But now it all came back mightily upon me out of the splendid stillness. It was not the written poem that I first remembered, but the one I only dreamed in those glorious, dedicated days that were made sacred by it, the white nights of heightened being when I *knew,* past saying and past singing.

With a full heart I lifted my voice to the listening silence, shouting lines remembered from the written poem.

Echoless, they died upon the empty air, and I was conscious of the biting cold again.

Sometime before the new day whitened, I was home.

81

I taught four months that winter, four the next, and two between terms, beginning when the corn was laid by and ending when the husking of it started. The shorter session was a bonus for the big boys, who maybe needed brushing up in their reading, figuring, spelling, and such before the winter session.

More and more after that night on the starry hilltop I had thought about the precious little book I'd written under the fancied shadow of impending death — a humble offering to the world in partial payment for a few earthly needs and the privilege of living here awhile. But my task remained unfinished so long as the work lay hidden in manuscript. Somehow I must see it into print and binding, a regular book among books — and what a thrilling thought that was!

So I began looking about for the names and addresses of publishers. Bowen-Merrill of Indianapolis seemed most promising, being publishers for the popular poet, James Whitcomb Riley. Wouldn't it be wonderful if . . . if only . . . ?

By now I had left schoolteaching for a job as stenographer and bookkeeper in Wayne, and the letter I sent with that manuscript must have been a work of art. I spent most of the spare time I could find for a week in composing and typing that letter.

At long last regrets and thanks came back from Indianapolis. My debt lay upon me heavier than ever.

Several weeks passed before I could generate hope enough for another try. This time it was James T. White & Co. of New York, publishers of *The National Cyclopedia of American Biography*. There was no reason whatever for the choice. Having seen the name for the first time, I had tossed a penny for a decision and it turned up heads!

The reply presented a dilemma. My poem had been read "with pleasure and admiration." They never published poetry on a royalty basis, but they would be pleased to undertake a trial edition of five hundred copies for the sum of two hundred dollars, which was little more than the cost of production and handling.

For a while I walked on air. "Pleasure and admiration"! But after all, two hundred dollars offered a formidable hurdle, being more money that I had ever seen assembled in one place. So near the shining goal, and yet so very far away! What could be done?

I presented the situation to my Uncle George, a tenant farmer in a time when corn and hogs were much cheaper than dollars and cents. But, bless his heart, he found an answer. The Wayne State Bank would take my note *without interest* for two years, if he would sign with me!

And so it was my little book was born!

82

It was such a lovely little book—forty-six neatly printed pages of it, sumptuously bound in brilliant golden buckram. It was hard to believe, but there it was on the title page:

THE DIVINE ENCHANTMENT

A Mystical Poem

by
J. G. Neihardt

The excitement greatly increased when review notices began coming in from the outside world. Most of the notices were, of course, perfunctory, with little understanding; some few, irreverently sarcastic or jocose. But there were others that dealt seriously with the ambitious little volume and in kindly fashion, finding inevitable faults but also "notable achievement and much promise."

By and by the flow of comment trickled to a stop, and the old familiar world of prose came plodding back, uncaring and unchanged. Like the lines I shouted to the listening stillness on a starry hilltop, it seemed my masterpiece had fallen echoless on empty air.

Still, in many a solitary session with it, I knew again the poem it was meant to be—and sometimes almost was. But more and more the faults stood out in brazen nakedness to mock me, until I almost feared to read. And more and more the soundless voice that came to me in boyhood seemed calling me again. *There was something to be overtaken—Come away, come away!*

It all ended, so far as this world may know, with a roaring bonfire in our back yard. For hours John and I fed *Divine Enchantments* to the flames; and those that survived the sacrificial fire, save only a score, were given later to the cookstove. I remember there was heartache in the act, for yonder was the funeral pyre of my youth and all the dreams that were too big for doing. But there was triumph too; for I knew that I was growing, and endings now were all beginnings. Freed from alien eyes and cleansed of all its faults as by the fire divine, I liked to fancy that somehow my little book was perfect now forever — the book I tried to make it.

For fifty years I did not open it again.

ALL
IS BUT A
BEGINNING

———◦∞◦———

This episodic story of my boyhood and youth is offered as a token of heartfelt greeting to the young of the much discussed present generation. Many of those may know me, by my *Black Elk Speaks, A Cycle of the West,* or television appearances perhaps, as a spiritual comrade in this amazing earthly adventure of ours. Happily there is no "gap" between us; for it will be noted that my somewhat garrulous rememberings alternate freely between tears and laughter, and I am therefore not unacquainted with the hardships and hilarities incidental to growing up in a world notoriously out of joint.

This "younger generation" in which I claim honorary membership, regardless of my years, is caught up in the greatest social revolution the world has ever known. Discord and violence are commonplace the world over. Throughout the realm of human values the raucous yawp of anarchy is loud. In wide, densely populated areas of the planet abject misery and chronic terror are ways of life; sordid systematic killing a thriving industry, its success measured by the daily bag of "enemy" dead. It is no wonder that our youngsters would reject the mad world they have inherited. Surely there is more than frivolity and fashion in their hirsute excesses, more than clowning in their irreverence for the Established and the smug.

Do the laughing gods poke cruel fun at us?

But for all the scornful nose-thumbings at the discarded past, the discredited present, and the mistrusted future, a most hopeful sign is to be noted. Among these dissident youngsters there is an upward surge of spiritual longing. Apparently they are seeking a new, direct approach to a viable religion. Even the resort to drugs must be regarded as an attempted shortcut to the desired mystical experience.

As a university lecturer I was intimately and happily associated with young people for some years. They always seemed to be more earnestly questioning than hopeful; less joyous, and older than young people should be.

"What's it all about?" and "What's good about it?" were characteristic and often-recurring questions. They still are, especially now that I have attained this snow-topped summit of my heaped-up ninety years and more. Surely, those young people must think, having come so far and climbed so high, he must have learned some of the vital answers.

But "What's it all about?" Ask God that question. He won't tell; and if He did we would not understand. Anyway, to ask that question is to die a little. No doubt even a tree would wither if it got to thinking what the summers and the winters meant.

But "What's good about it?" That is indeed an important question, and it admits an answer. It has plagued me, too, in my darker moods.

I have a formal garden, hedge-enclosed, where I often go to pray and seek for needed answers. However the faith-inspired religionist or the scientific psychologist may explain the mechanism of prayer, I have found it a rewarding practice; and I suspect that it may be vastly more powerful than we know.

There are times when I enter my garden not to worship but just to *be*—and listen. It is such a time that I now recall. I was thinking lamely of the world's multitudinous woes, including some minor ones of my own, when the shadowy form of a cynical young friend of mine floated across my consciousness. I fancied him pressing the troublesome question upon me: "What's good about this absurd predicament in which we find ourselves? We don't know whence we came; we don't know where we are; we don't know whither we are bound. It is hard to come here, hard to remain, and sometimes very hard to get away."

I listened, and the answer came out of the silence:

"Four things, at least, are good," I found myself replying.

"First: Surely love is good—love given rather than love received. With neither, there is nothing; with either, even sorrow and suffering may become beautiful and dear. All good things come from love, and it is the only thing that is increased by giving it away.

"Second: The satisfaction of the instinct of workmanship is good; for that instinct is the noblest thing in man after love, from which indeed it springs. Just to do your best at any cost, and afterward to experience something of the Seventh Day glory when you look upon your work and see that it is good.

"Third: The exaltation of expanded awareness in moments of spiritual insight is good. This may occur in a flash, glorifying the world; or it may linger for days, when you seem to float above all worldly troubling, and all faces become familiar and dear. This state can be spontaneously generated, but it has often been achieved through fasting and prayer.

"Fourth: Deep sleep is good.

"'Not shoaling slumber, but the ocean-deep
And dreamless sort,'

as one of my characters in *The Song of Jed Smith* remarks.

"'There's something that you touch,
And what you call it needn't matter much
If you can reach it. Call it only rest,
And there is something else you haven't guessed—
The Everlasting, maybe. You can try
To live without it, but you have to die
Back into it a little now and then.
And maybe praying is a way for men

To reach it when they cannot sleep a wink
For trouble.'"

For some time I continued to mull over the implications of the answer. Then I was struck by the realization that both my cynical young friend and I were of necessity concerned with fragmentary conceptions; that each "good" that I had offered involved the loss of the sense of self in some pattern larger than self; that life, as commonly conceived, could be only a fragment of some vaster pattern; and that prayer itself was a striving to be whole.

There is a slogan that I wish to leave with my young friends to be recalled for courage, like a battle cry, in times of great stress. It came to me from an old Sioux friend of mine who was recounting his experience as a youth on Vision Quest.

He had fasted three days and nights upon a lonely hill, praying all the while that Wakon Tonka might send him a vision. But his prayer got lost, far out in the empty night, and it seemed that nothing heard.

Then, on the fourth day, he fell asleep, exhausted, and dreamed a troubled dream that had no glory in it. Any old woman could have dreamed it, nidding and nodding in her tepee. He wakened in despair. And as he stood forlorn upon his hilltop he was thinking: If I have no vision to give me power and guide me, how can I ever be a man? Maybe I shall have to go far off into a strange land and seek an enemy to free me from this shame.

Then, just as he thought this bitter thought, a great cry came from overhead like a fearless warrior hailing his wavering comrade in heat of battle. "Hoka-hey, brother — *Hold fast, hold fast; there is more!*" Looking up, he saw an eagle soaring yonder on a spread of mighty wings — and it was the eagle's voice he heard.

"As I listened," the old man said, "a power ran through me that has never left me, old as I am. Often when it seemed the end had come, I have heard the eagle's cry — *Hold fast, hold fast; there is more. . . .*"